The Awful Truth Cleaning Products And Fertility Revealed

BY
GABRIELA ROSA

ASSOCIATE PUBLISHING

The Awful Truth About Cleaning Products And Fertility
Revealed

By Gabriela Rosa

ISBN-13: 978-0-9788010-9-0
ISBN-10: 0-9788010-9-1

Cover design by Embrace Design Solutions.
www.embracedesigns.com.au

Made in the United States of America

Get Your FREE Bonuses Today!

FREE Fertility Advice from 'The Bringer of Babies'

Leading natural fertility specialist, Gabriela Rosa (aka The Bringer of Babies) has a gift for you. As a thank you for purchasing this book get your FREE "Natural Fertility Booster" subscription and discover...

- Easy ways to comprehensively boost your fertility and conceive naturally, even for women over 40;
- Natural methods to dramatically increase your chances of creating a baby through assisted reproductive technologies such as IUI, IVF, GIFT or ICSI;
- Simple strategies to help you take home a healthier baby;
- How to prevent miscarriages.

You will also receive the FREE audio CD "11 Proven Steps To Create The Pregnancy You Desire And Take Home The Healthy Baby of Your Dreams" a total value of $397!

Claim your bonuses at
www.NaturalFertilityBoost.com

Be quick, this is a limited offer.
(Your free subscription code is: ATCP)

Gabriela Rosa can be contacted via
www.BoostYourFertilityNow.com

Attention Gabriela Rosa

PO Box 2342

Bondi Junction NSW 1355

Australia

Dedication

To my loving husband Maurice and our own future creations.

About the Author

Leading natural fertility specialist and naturopath Gabriela Rosa has gained international recognition as an expert in her field. Gabriela is the founder of Natural Fertility & Health Solutions—a multi-modality, integrative medicine centre based in Sydney, Australia. She dedicates herself to the management of women's health issues (from puberty to menopause), men's health and natural fertility treatment.

Gabriela is the author of *Eat your Way to Parenthood: The Diet Secrets of Highly Fertile Couples Revealed (2008), The Awful Truth About Cleaning Products and Fertility Revealed (2008)* and *Protecting Your Fertility—The Dangers Of Conventional Pest Control and Natural, Safe Alternatives Revealed (2008)* available from Amazon.com and all major bookstores worldwide. She has been featured in major Australian newspapers such as *The Daily Telegraph* and magazines such as *Woman's Day*. Gabriela has contributes to various radio programs in Australia and overseas, including Mix 106.5, 2UE, ABC and LA radio and she currently has a regular spot on Sydney radio.

In 2001, Gabriela created the highly successful **Natural Fertility Solution Program,** which she and her team run from her Sydney practice. With the aim of taking the program to couples all over the world, in 2008 Gabriela produced **The Natural Fertility Solution Take-Home Program**, which assists couples in overcoming fertility problems and provides them with the best possible chance of creating a healthy baby. The program is based on Gabriela's *11 Pillars of Fertility,* shown to dramatically increase a couples chances of a natural conception, while reducing the likelihood of miscarriage. The program has also shown to increase the odds for couples undergoing *in vitro* fertilization (IVF) procedures. Gabriela's program isn't just for couples with fertility problems—it's an essential toolkit for those who simply wish to prepare for the healthiest conception and baby.

Gabriela lives in Sydney with her husband.

Acknowledgements

I would like to thank and dedicate this book to all those people who throughout my life believed in me and for the lessons that made me grow beyond my wildest imagination. There are so many people to mention that this whole books would not be enough, however I would like to specially thank and acknowledge the following people:

Brook Canning, Vivienne Weinstock, Paul Doney and Paul Bayley—the incredible team at Natural Fertility & Health Solutions—without your support and friendship especially over the last year this project would probably still be unfinished! I am honoured to work with such amazing Integrative Medicine Practitioners as yourselves; To Carolina Silva, Gail Anne Waid, Carol Witt and Emma French without you this work would not be what it is today—I am eternally grateful for your support, your diligence and your tremendous ability to so beautifully transform my ideas into concrete reality; My family—mum, dad and Dani because you are my world and you continue to teach me so much about focus and determination; To my wonderful husband Maurice for your unwavering encouragement and delightful spirit—You are such a marvellous companion and I feel so fortunate to share my life with you; To Fofs because you are a massive cheering squad in such a tiny package; To Horton and Rishi, for bringing such fun and laughter into our lives! To Margaret and Aaron for being like my second parents—I love you both! To my new family Rosy, Michel, Marcel, and Michal thank you for helping me grow. And of course I couldn't forget to thank and appreciate my friends, teachers and mentors, present and past who even in the smallest ways continue to help, guide and encourage me to share the gift of optimum health and fertility with the world through their diverse and very special contributions: Dr Jim Ferry, Dr Jeff Jankelson, Francesca Naish, Jane Challinor, Mal Emery, Greg Owen and Wayne Pickstone.

Finally, my love to the future beneficiaries of this work and the gift of life—the babies I help bring into the world; through the loving intentions and consistent efforts of devoted and caring prospective parents who are touched by my message.

Foreword

I first met Gabriela Rosa in 2002 and was overwhelmed by the positive attitude, enthusiasm and sincerity with which she approaches her work. It was as evident then, as it is now, how very passionate she is about what she does. Gabriela combines the art and science of naturopathy with her genuine wish to help her patients by educating, empowering and encouraging them to take responsibility for their health. Gabriela is very compassionate and professional, yet she brings a little bit of magic to all who meet her.

I was therefore thrilled to hear that she was writing a series of books for prospective parents on how to optimise fertility by taking care of one's general health and reducing exposure to chemicals including those in pest control and cleaning products.

It seems that every week we read of a link between chemicals and illness, including allergies, behavioural problems and cancer. It has been estimated that over 80,000 synthetic chemicals, many of them poisonous to our biological systems, have been developed over the past 50 years. Each year, 2,000 to 3,000 new chemicals are brought to the US Environmental Protection Agency for review before manufacture. Governments can be slow to act and industry often rates immediate profit above consumer health. The problem is compounded by the length of time these substances persist in our environment, as well as the issues of bio-accumulation and bio-magnification. Furthermore, growing humans with their smaller size and developing detoxification mechanisms are more susceptible to the effects of these chemicals than adults. Injury to developing organ systems can cause lifelong disability.

Combinations of chemicals can have effects that are more damaging than individual chemicals alone. The effects on future generations of humans and other animals remain to be seen. As we cannot ethically perform trials on humans and observe and document these effects, do we really know the full extent of the problem? This issue is compounded both by the lag time from exposure to onset of illness, as well as the sheer number of foreign molecules we are exposed to on a daily basis.

The most sensible thing we can do is to educate ourselves. By revealing the awful truth about conventional cleaning products, this book provides a wealth of information as well as practical solutions for the everyday problem of keeping our homes healthy. It is packed full of commonsense information on environmentally, and fertility-friendly cleaning, including where to buy the affordable, natural ingredients and step-by-step instructions on how to make your own products. Gabriela's comprehensive, yet easy to understand, advice is presented in her positive, motivational style and includes great information on how to save time and effort whilst optimising your health and fertility. This wonderful reference book is a must-have for every 21st century bookshelf—whether you are planning on conceiving or not. I know I will enjoy it for years to come.

Dr Hilary Stevenson MBChB, FRACGP

-Integrative General Practitioner—YourHealth Manly, Sydney

-Member of the Australasian College of Nutritional & Environmental Medicine

An Additional Note from Dr Emmanuel Varipatis

To introduce the topic of toxic chemicals, pesticides and children's health I am going to first make the statement that "babies are being born polluted"

There is new research recently published which indicates that there is a linear correlation between tissue levels of pesticides and the incidence of insulin resistance. I will discuss this research to demonstrate an important point.

We first need to understand that insulin resistance is the new 'epidemic' metabolic disorder that has been creating the worldwide tsunami wave of obesity and diabetes and all the eventual complications of these two conditions.

It is commonly known that obesity with related diabetes can be traced back to genetics plus a high GI diet. It is simple, eat too many sweets, white bread, and donuts as a child, and end up fat and eventually diabetic.

However, we now have research that shows that just being born with high levels of various chemical compounds (including those found in conventional cleaning products) in your bloodstream, will damage the hormonal system and cause insulin resistance. You could become obese and diabetic as a child, and sick and disabled as an adult, despite being brought up by parents who were careful to give you a healthy balanced diet, and despite a lifetime of 'doing the right thing'. Your parents just need to have been exposed to chemicals during their life and have accumulated tissue residues that can be passed on to you, as a baby in-utero and through breast-feeding. These chemicals then permanently damage sensitive developing systems.

Now, for the first time in history, children are being born with pre-existing levels of synthetic chemicals in their bodies. Of the hundred thousand plus chemicals involved, only a handful have ever been tested for toxicity effects on foetuses, and the handful that were tested, all demonstrated the ability to cause severe damage in some form. There was then a prolonged battle fought for years with the vested interests involved in these chemicals which blocked any regulation or restriction of their products.

Think tobacco; think asbestos or lead; and now think mercury, bisphenol-A, phthalates and antimony in children's clothing and bedding. Then wonder about the other 100,000 plus chemicals that have not even made it into the scientific spotlight or into the media.

A study was recently done in the US on the cord blood of newly born babies. They looked for a range of known toxins and found the majority were present AT BIRTH in the cord blood collected. Of these, 62% were known carcinogens, 75% were neuro-devolopmentally toxic, and many were known to produce birth defects or reproductive system damage.

Hence the statement **"babies are being born polluted"**

This counts as the biggest experiment ever conducted on humans, and one in which the results are unknown, but likely not to be pretty.

There is currently no system in place around the world to make manufacturers test chemicals for foetal and neo-natal impact. On the few occasions products are tested, it is on lab animals and on healthy young adults. We do not have a 'safety first' policy, and after these chemicals are released it may take decades before the damaging effects become known and action finally taken. By this stage, every living thing on earth will have measurable tissue levels of persistent organic pollutants (POPs).

In-utero development, which amazingly converts one single cell into a complex human being of 10 trillion cells, involves the DNA of the one original cell directing an impossibly complex production process. All the research indicates that this process is easily disrupted in-utero and in the neonate.

This probably explains the changes currently seen in paediatric diseases. Up to only a few generations ago, the challenge facing children was to survive the high incidence of deaths in childbirth and then to survive malnutrition-related and infection-related deaths in early childhood. Once past these barriers, the surviving children were generally fit and healthy.

Today this has all changed. In most countries infant mortality is low, and we are now faced with epidemics of new paediatric conditions that were not present only a few years ago.

The new face of childhood diseases is that of...

- Allergies, Epipens and nut-free schools

- Asthma

- ADHD and other learning and behavioural problems

- Autism

- Paediatric cancers

- Schools full of overweight, sickly children who, as adults, will have high incidences of infertility, obesity, diabetes, hypertension, heart disease, Alzheimer's, Parkinson's, infertility, cancer, mood disorders and so on.

There is no doubt that this is the world in which we now live.

If we change the way we do things, so that development, industry, economics and agriculture become 'sustainable' and eco-friendly, then perhaps we will give the next generation the best possible chance for a healthy body and brain.

Until then, Gabriela Rosa's advice is of critical importance. To give your child the best chance then parents (and prospective parents) need to make their bodies as healthy as possible, and the home needs to be as chemical-free as possible.

In toxicology, the rule always is that the best treatment is that of prevention. Much easier to keep chemicals out of our bodies, and therefore out of our babies, than to try and remove them once they have found their way in.

Dr Emmanuel Varipatis MB.BS. (UNSW)

-Integrative General Practitioner—YourHealth Manly, Sydney.

-Fellow of the Australasian College of Nutritional & Environmental Medicine (FACNEM)

-Board-Certifi ed Clinical Metal Toxicologist (IBCMT)

-Founding Board member MINDD Foundation

-Board-certifi ed with "Defeat Autism Now" of Autism research Institute, USA

Contents

Introduction

A healthy, unpolluted and non-toxic environment is essential for optimum fertility. Everything in our macro and micro environment impacts on our health and fertility. Chemicals damage our health and have a huge impact on the Earth's delicate ecosystems. So, it's not surprising that they end up impacting on the maturation of healthy sperm and eggs, the basis of healthy embryos. That is why it is so important that you make positive changes (ideally, beginning at least 120 days prior to a conception attempt), in order to overcome fertility problems and have the healthiest possible baby.

Everything you are exposed to, or do, for at least 120 days prior to a conception attempt will have huge repercussions on your ability to conceive, but even more importantly will dramatically affect the health of your prospective child. Commonly-used cleaning chemicals are not only toxic, they also unbalance human hormonal levels because they mimic our hormones, particularly oestrogen, and end up blocking receptors for other hormones, such as testosterone. For women this is a problem because it enhances oestrogen dominance, leading to hormonal 'disproportion' and contributing to conditions such as endometriosis and fibroids as well as certain types of female reproductive cancers. For men it disrupts testosterone balance and therefore healthy sperm production. Hormonal imbalances also disrupt embryonic development, particularly in regards to sexual development and reproductive function later in life. As you will see, by simply changing your cleaning habits, you can safeguard your health and the health of your prospective family!

From the outset, however, I must be clear that although every positive change is very important, each is but a single piece of the optimum fertility puzzle. Only together can they generate the necessary synergy to create profound and positive change. A whole person approach, taking all the pieces of the puzzle into consideration, is the essential way to restore and optimise natural fertility in men or women.

I have identified 11 key areas making up the platform I named the 11 Pillars of Fertility, which underpins my natural fertility treatment approach. In order to create the result many couples yearn for: The baby of their dream—these key areas require diligent ad simultaneous implementation.

One of these important areas addresses the need to avoid toxic exposure to chemicals such as pesticides in order to truly optimise a couple's fertility as well as safeguard the health of a prospective child, hence the value of this book.

Fertility is not an isolated 'event'—it is intrinsically connected with emotional, whole body and even (believe it or not) spiritual health. The body and the spirit are constantly striving towards balance, good health, fertility, energy and happiness. The problem is that due to our hectic lifestyles, health compromises and poor daily choices, we often overlook the basic requirements for incredible health and optimum fertility.We only take care of ourselves when something breaks down rather than making daily choices that maintain our most precious possession to the absolute best of our ability.

Thankfully, given the right circumstances, the human body is capable of seemingly miraculous shifts. It takes sufficient time, energy, nutrients, lifestyle changes and other desirable conditions, but at any time, the choice is yours. You can choose to take the time to listen to your body, to learn from it and work with it.

There are empowering and endless possibilities, even in cases where all hope had previously been lost.

Frequently we hear of 'miracles' happening in other people's lives. The key to making it happen is the belief in the possibility it can. True belief in these possibilities creates a change in attitude and mindset, which in turn makes you want to seek out further information and knowledge. This leads to a change in behaviour, which in turn creates different results and shapes your new reality.

Believe in possibilities, but do more—make the commitment to truly take the time to make friends with and nurture your body, as you would nurture your newborn baby—irrespective of any outcome, because it is only in doing so, that no matter what happens, you will create new possibilities for yourself and, who knows, hopefully even the baby of your dreams.

I have guided many couples using this approach and it has proven very successful for overcoming fertility problems, preventing miscarriages and increasing the chances of taking home a healthy baby— preventing miscarriages and malformation (even for older couples). However this is not its only application, it is also a vitally important approach for any prospective parents who simply wish to prepare for the healthiest possible conception and baby, giving a child the best possible start in life.

My patients are proof. I remember one couple who had had many complications and two stillbirths prior to seeing me. They implemented my recommendations and went on to have a healthy baby. They summed it up best when they said: "A healthy baby is 'a hope', not 'a promise'. Hope must be underpinned by specific actions and positive preparation and even then, it is not entirely in our hands. But knowing we've done our part and the very best we could means we can now relax." Helping you do your part, and the very best you can, towards fulfilling your dream of a healthy baby, is what this book is all about.

In this book you will learn how you can clean using safe, natural, chemical-free, non-toxic ingredients, which will slash your supermarket and cleaning product bills—because as an extra benefit, they are really inexpensive! You will also learn how to safeguard your environment for your and your family's safety—and you will be doing the Earth a great favour too!

I hope you enjoy this healthy, original way of cleaning. Remember to experiment and have fun—your health, fertility and the environment will thank you!

With Love and Fertile Blessings,

Gabriela Rosa aka 'The Bringer of Babies'
BHSc, ND, Post Grad NFM, DBM, Dip Nut, MATMS, MNHAA
www.BoostYourFertilityNow.com

Chemicals and
Their Impact on
Fertility and Health

Gabriela Rosa

Chemicals and Their Impact on Fertility and Health

"Chemicals have replaced bacteria and viruses as the main threat to health. The diseases we are beginning to see as the major causes of death in the latter part of (the 1900's) and into the 21st century are diseases of chemical origin."

--Dr. Dick Irwin, Toxicologist, Texas A&M University

Most of us are oblivious to the ways in which the chemical compounds and substances we encounter affect our fertility and reproductive health. They are just part of everyday life. You might pop on some latex gloves when using a caustic cleaning product, or give your hands an extra-thorough wash after using one, but do you ever consider avoiding them altogether? And how often do you connect your contact with everyday household cleaners with your fertility? We don't consider such things normally, but if you are having difficulties in starting a family, it brings your daily lifestyle under sharp scrutiny.

Commonsense tells you to limit your exposure to seriously toxic chemicals, but what does cleaning the bathroom have to do with your fertility? Well, the answer to that lies in the effect that commercial cleaning and other commonly-used products have on human hormones.

REPRODUCTIVE HORMONES

Your fertility is controlled by the action of hormones. Any disruption in the function of these hormones can affect your reproductive future. Over the past few years, many common chemicals in homes and in the environment have been found to affect human health. Researchers and scientists have identified ways that man-made, and even naturally occurring, chemicals can influence fertility by imitating the action of hormones.

Hormones are chemical substances that act as the messengers of the endocrine system. This is a complex system of glands and hormones that regulates and controls many of the body's functions. Hormones influence functions such as reproduction, growth, development and maturation, as well as regulating the metabolism of various organs. Endocrine glands (including the adrenal, thyroid, pituitary, thymus, pancreas, ovaries, and testes) manufacture hormones and deposit them directly into the bloodstream, which carries them around the body to control and regulate various metabolic and physiological activities. Hormones are generally classed as peptides (for example insulin and ADH [anti-diuretic hormone]), or steroids (such as testosterone and progesterone).

Hormonal Balance

The endocrine glands that control reproduction are the ovaries in females and the testes in males. The testes make testosterone, which stimulates characteristics in men such as facial hair, increased muscle, broad shoulders and the development of the male reproductive system.

In females, there are several hormones that affect fertility. The first, FSH or follicle stimulating hormone is produced by the pituitary gland. This hormone prompts the ovaries into maturing eggs and producing oestrogen. Next, the pituitary gland releases a surge of luteinizing hormone or LH, which causes the ovary to release the mature egg. LH is the hormone that ovulation predictor kits detect.

The ovaries produce oestrogen and progesterone. Together, these hormones are responsible for the development and maturation of the inner lining of the uterus called the endometrium to which a fertilised egg attaches. Oestrogen also causes the cervical fluid to be thin and abundant and the basal body temperature to drop at ovulation—important requirements for conceiving. Progesterone is the hormone released after ovulation by the corpus luteum and is responsible for raising the basal body temperature (post ovulation) and preparing the uterine lining whilst it awaits implantation of a fertilised egg. After a fertilised egg has implanted itself into the uterine lining, the developing embryo produces the hormone HCG, or human chorionic gonadotropin. This hormone is also known as the pregnancy hormone and can be detected with a pregnancy test. HCG helps to maintain the corpus luteum, which maintains the high levels of progesterone to further develop the endometrium lining. In conjunction with a healthy functioning thyroid gland, progesterone also helps to keep basal temperatures high for the optimum development of the embryo in the early stages of pregnancy.

How Hormones Work

This delicate balance of hormones works on a messenger/receptor system. Specialised cells are receptive to the hormone messengers. Their surfaces contain receptor sites designed to fit a particular messenger. When a hormone locks into its receptor on a cell surface, it triggers the cell to initiate functions such as prompting the ovary to mature and release eggs. A common analogy for the messenger/receptor system is to think of the cell as a lock and the hormone as a key. Certain keys can only fit into certain locks. Even though a cell has receptors on its surface, if a key passes by in the bloodstream that doesn't fit the lock, the cell ignores it. If a key fits, however, it connects itself to its slot in the cell surface and delivers its message.

Hormones are very powerful chemicals. They are so powerful that measurement of their presence in the bloodstream is expressed in parts per trillion. If too much of any hormone is present in the bloodstream it can cause problems for the body. Because of this, a receptor cell must notify the endocrine gland that it has received its delivery of hormones and therefore does not require any more. The body uses this feedback system to regulate and control certain functions in the body. As well as the reproductive hormones, nearly every type of organ and tissue also produces hormones each with its own message. They control not only reproduction, but also growth, development, and other important functions. It is a very effective system but one that can very easily be disrupted.

Hormone Disrupters

Research from around the world confirms many chemicals are known human endocrine disruptors including those used in plasticisers (plastics), pesticides, fungicides, herbicides, industrial and household products as well as even some personal hygiene items.

The problem is that the structure of these chemicals is so similar to certain hormones that they appear to receptor cells as hormone look-alikes. These impostors will lock onto a receptor site, but because they are not really the hormones intended for the cell, they will block a correct message or deliver an incorrect message signalling the cell to do the wrong things. They may alter normal hormone levels, stop or start hormone production, change the way in which hormones travel through the body or even change hormonal functions. They may even turn functions off or on at the wrong times, or alter the level of importance of the message. These chemicals cause havoc on many levels and consequently may have a direct, negative impact on one's health and fertility. Endocrine disruption as it relates to reproduction and general health due to man-made toxic exposure is currently a primary area of research.

Gabriela Rosa

ENDOCRINE-DISRUPTING CHEMICALS (EDCS) AND THE ENVIRONMENT

In general exposure to EDCs can occur through direct contact or through drinking contaminated water, ingesting tainted food, or even breathing the air. Outdoors, they occur naturally in the soil and in some plants. They are also found in agricultural chemicals and some household products such as insecticides, herbicides, fumigants, fungicides, cleaning products and personal hygiene items.

Endocrine disruptors can be a by-product of many chemical and manufacturing processes. They enter the air or water when plastics and other materials are burned and there is although some indication that they can leach out of plastics in landfill.

It is suspected that EDCs accumulate in fat, so eating fatty foods and fish from contaminated waste may increase exposure to EDCs. Babies are thought to ingest them through breast milk and during development in their mother's womb.

New information is continually becoming available about common natural compounds and synthetic chemicals that are used, disposed of, or excreted by people or animals and consequently end up in storm run-off and wastewater. Even though wastewater treatment removes a considerable amount of these chemicals, tiny concentrations of some are still discharged with the treated water.

The health risks associated with constant exposures to low levels of these chemicals are still largely unknown and highly controversial. Changes can range from subtle differences in normal hormone levels in the bloodstream to infertility, abnormalities in reproductive systems, or even cancer. The best course of action is to avoid them wherever possible.

It should be noted, however that many of these chemicals are present at low levels throughout our environment, so totally avoiding them is impossible, however making better choices in our day to day will reduce your direct exposure. Buying less 'products' of all types (personal or household) and choosing less packaging for your food is best.

"Cancer rates have continued to increase every year since 1970. Brain cancer in children is up 40% in 20 years. Toxic chemicals are largely to blame."

—*NY Times, September 29, 1997*

SOME WELL-KNOWN EDCS

A vast range of chemical groups and compounds has been used in many products over the years. It is now suggested that on average, there are over four million chemical mixtures in our immediate home and business environments, most of which unfortunately carry little information on the risks posed to health and fertility. Due to such varied exposure combinations, ill effects are usually difficult to isolate. In addition chemicals can also be naturally occurring, or in a form beyond human detection or control—as a result the real danger of many chemicals are not isolated or thoroughly investigated. Hence the exposure to known dangerous compounds (which can be avoided in one's immediate environment) tends to be more significant than we often realise or are led to believe.

The common chemical groups and compounds discussed in this section are found in commercial cleaning products or leached into them due to the types of containers used for their storage. In other cases, the information provided serves as an example of the damaging, yet usually unknown effects of certain chemicals (frequently man-made) present in our environment—and how sometimes following an 'accepted' way of thinking is not in your best interest or that of your prospective children. In most cases when it comes to commercial cleaning agents, although nowadays highly accepted as 'The only way' to clean—upon further questioning and exploration one soon realises the danger in a seemingly inoffensive decision—either way there is extensive research linking the substances presented here to health, fertility and reproductive problems in both animals and humans.

The tragedy about most dangerous chemical substances to which we are exposed, including those found in household cleaning agents, is that often their effects are not known until they have created a large number of victims. The key to safeguarding your health and fertility is this: If you are unsure about the safety of a particular product or in the event its safety information is inconclusive—you are best to avoid it completely. No law requires manufacturers of cleaning products to list ingredients on their labels or to test their products for safety. Generally, as a simple rule of thumb when it comes to commercial household cleaning products if the ingredients are not clearly labeled, and they contain explicit 'DANGER, WARNING and POISON warnings' and/or exalt strong (symptom-causing) fumes the product highly likely contains toxic substances which can and will affect your health and fertility.

Be cautious about marketing hype. Any manufacturer that claim to be environmentally friendly but does not disclose a full list of ingredients or has warning labels all over their product more often than not are not telling the whole story.

"According to the National Research Council, no toxic information is available for more than 80% of the chemicals in everyday-use products.

Only 1% of toxins are required to be listed on labels, because companies classify their formulas as "trade secrets."

—*Lorie Dwornick, researcher, educator and activist,*
2002

In addition, although most chemical studies are carried out on animals, typically their conclusions can for the most part be interpreted and extrapolated onto humans. In this section, this overview of the best-known EDCs is intended to provide a helpful resource and includes the following information for each chemical or group:

- Chemical Name and Description

- Environmental Occurrence

- Health Risks to Adults

- Health Risks to Children and Effect on Fertility

- Avoiding Exposure

Bisphenol A (BPA)

BPA is used in making polycarbonate plastics and epoxy resins. It was introduced back in 1891 and was researched heavily in the 1930s with a view to using it as a synthetic oestrogen because of its oestrogen-like properties. However, another synthetic oestrogen called diethylstilbestrol was found to be more powerful than even natural oestrogen, and development of BPA as a synthetic oestrogen was discontinued. Instead, it was utilised as a polymerisation agent for plastics, particularly polycarbonates. These plastics are widely used for products such as sunglasses and CDs because they are temperature resistant, impact resistant and have optical properties. One widely-used application for BPA is in food and water containers, cooking utensils and 'unbreakable' baby bottles. This last category has caused them to come under increased scrutiny because of their EDC properties. BPA has also been used in epoxy resins, specifically in the coatings used for the inside of food cans, and as an ingredient in dental fillings.

Environmental Occurrence:

It has been found that BPA tends to leach into the environment from food can linings and most commercial cleaning product containers (released into your immediate environment either through fume or residue exposure when such products are used). BPA also leaches out if plastics containing it are used in microwaves or subjected to very hot water, harsh detergents, or acidic liquids. Unfortunately, the baby bottles for which this chemical is used are usually washed in very hot water (and sterilised) with tough detergents. They are also often filled with highly acidic liquids such as juices. This combination of release mechanisms can result in an increased risk to babies who drink out of these bottles and adults who use plastics in their day to day.

Health Risks to Adults:

BPA is a well-known EDC that imitates oestrogen and initiates effects in the body similar to natural estrogens. Since research conducted in the 1930s, reports have confirmed the hormone-disrupting properties of this substance. Studies on human cancer cells show that even very low levels of the chemical can trigger these problems. When exposure occurs during growth and development, BPA can increase the likelihood of developing health problems such as cancer (including male and female reproductive types e.g. breast, uterine and ovarian for women and prostate for men), developmental delays and possible toxicity to nerve cells.

There is continuing controversy about BPA, with government agencies in many countries re-evaluating the health risks to humans and initiating new safety studies.

Health risks to children and effect on fertility:

BPA has been linked to changes in breast tissue and permanent changes to the reproductive system, as well as gender confusion in both males and females. It is also considered a carcinogen, In addition, behavioural changes, such as hyperactivity and a reduced display of maternal behaviour, have been observed.

In females these compounds can also lead to hormonal imbalances which can result in fertility problems. During pregnancy they can lead the feminisation of the male embryo causing reproductive development problems and in adult males, exposure has been shown to affect the prostate and lower production of testosterone in the body, which are known to result in sperm defects including lowered sperm count as well as poor shape and swimming abilities.

Because babies and children are growing and developing, any source of increased exposure to BPA should be of concern. Adults and infants consuming canned foods or infant formula from polycarbonate bottles will be ingesting increased concentrations of BPA.

Avoiding exposure:

Until studies conclusively prove otherwise, limit your contact with BPA-containing products, to protect your fertility and your family's health, and especially children. Avoid all canned foods and instead of using canned formula for infants, choose products that are packaged using other materials—where possible choose glass packaging.

"Of chemicals commonly found in homes, 150 have been linked to allergies, birth defects, cancer, and psychological disorders."

—**Consumer Protection Agency, United States**

Dioxin or Chlorinated Dibenzo-p-dioxins (CDDs)

CDDs are a group of 75 chemicals that have been shown to build up in wildlife in the environment and are ingested by humans who eat contaminated animal products such as fish, dairy products and meats. They are linked to birth defects, and are considered to be carcinogenic.

Environmental Occurrence:

CDDs are widely found in the environment. In cleaning product these are found in any chlorine/bleach containing agents (almost all types cleaning products particularly bathroom and kitchen!), which can come in contact with foods (residues), be breathed in during cleaning or absorbed through the skin due to direct exposure or contact with residues—in the shower for example. CDDs may also be created as a by-product of industry, particularly paper mills, and can form during water treatment processes (hence the importance of drinking water filtered by a good quality carbon filter of at most 1 micron—i.e. the filtration system thickness). CDDs can also be released into the air from solid waste and industrial incinerators. Exposure to dioxins occurs primarily from eating food contaminated by the chemicals and contamination from cleaning agents. One chemical in this group has been shown to cause skin problems and may cause cancer.

Health Risks to Adults:

People exposed to large amounts of one of the chemicals in this group, 2, 3, 7, 8-TCDD, develop a skin condition called chloracne—acne-like lesions, which erupt on the face and upper body similar to regular acne. Other skin rashes and such problems as discolouration of skin and growth of excessive body hair have been attributed to exposure to high levels of this particular chemical. Other symptoms include liver damage, permanent or chronic problems with glucose metabolism and changes in hormone concentrations.

Research shows that animals exposed to CDDs have reproductive problems such as miscarriages, birth defects including kidney problems, bone deformities and weakened immune systems. Similar studies have not been conducted with humans, but some research suggests that exposure to CDDs can increase the risk of developing certain types of cancer and they are labelled as a carcinogen by the World Health Organization (WHO).

Health risks to children and affect on fertility:

The skin problem chloracne has been recorded in children exposed to high levels of this toxin, but its association with the development of other health problems is inconclusive. The reproductive implications are unknown, but cannot be disregarded because of studies showing birth defects and related reproductive problems in animals exposed to high levels of these chemicals.

Avoiding exposure:

To protect you and your family from exposure, avoid the use of commercial cleaning products, cook and consume only good quality filtered water, and wash your fruit and vegetables thoroughly (in filtered water) before consumption. In addition, do not allow children to play in the dirt near known hazardous waste sites. All family members should wash their hands thoroughly after being near such sites. Young children and nursing mothers should avoid eating food grown or produced near known hazardous wastes sites—buy certified organic or biodynamic produce only wherever possible.

- *Within 26 seconds after exposure to chemicals such as cleaning products, traces of these chemicals can be found in every organ in the body.*

- *More than 1.4 million Americans exposed to household chemicals were referred to poison control centers in 2001. Of these, 824,000 were children under 6 years.*

- *A New York sanitation worker was killed in 1998 when a hazardous liquid in household trash sprayed his face and clothes.*

- *At any given time, there is 3.36 million tons of household hazardous waste to contend with in our country.*

*—Chec's HealtheHouse,
the resource for Environmental
Health Risks Affecting Your Children*

Polychlorinated Biphenyls (PCBs)

PCBs are a combination of over 200 separate chemicals (some present in commercial cleaning agents and personal hygiene items). Prior to 1977 they were used as coolants and lubricants in electrical equipment such as capacitors and transformers, as they have good insulating properties and burn slowly. No natural sources of PCBs are known. They are usually odourless, tasteless oily substances and can occur as solids, liquids or gases.

Environmental Occurrence:

PCBs become airborne when manufactured and can enter the water and soil from spills and leaks during shipping. Products containing PCBs can melt or break in a fire, releasing these toxins into the environment, where they take a long time to break down. These compounds can also travel for miles on air currents, so contaminated areas can be much larger than expected. PCBs dissolve readily in water and remain suspended but they primarily bind to organic matter and settle to the bottom of bodies of water. They also stick strongly to soil.

Fish are particularly affected. Tiny fish and small organisms are consumed by larger creatures, and eventually by predatory creatures such as large fish and marine mammals that eat fish. In this way, PCBs can accumulate to levels far higher than those expected from simple exposure.

Health Risks to Adults:

It has been shown that PCBs collect in the environment and are implicated in health problems in humans and animals, so their use was discontinued in 1977. Products made before this time may still contain PCBs. Health problems in people who have been associated with exposure to PCBs include an acne-like or rash-like skin conditions in adults. Industrial workers exposed to high levels of PCBs can show subtle changes in blood and urine, indicating possible liver damage. In animals, exposure to PCBs has been associated with cancer.

Exposure to high levels of a PCB called toluene has been associated with kidney problems in humans. Studies show that industrial workers exposed to PCBs can develop cancer, primarily liver cancer and cancer of the biliary tract. PCBs are considered likely to be carcinogenic.

Health risks to children and effect on fertility:

Research shows that women who ate large amounts of contaminated fish or were exposed to PCBs in the workplace had babies with slightly lower birth weights than unaffected women. In addition, their babies showed abnormal test results for such things as behaviour, motor skills and short-term memory that endured for many years. Babies breastfed by exposed mothers could suffer problems with their immune system, and some studies indicated that babies could be exposed to PCBs across the placenta. However, mothers who are concerned about PCBs in breast milk should realise that the benefits of breastfeeding are thought to far outweigh any dangers from PCBs. PCBs are not linked to birth defects, nor found to cause problems in older children.

Studies on animals that ingested large amounts of PCBs over a short time have shown that some suffered liver damage and even death. Longer exposure to smaller amounts of the toxins resulted in the animals developing anaemia, skin disorders, and thyroid gland, stomach and liver damage. Behavioural changes were also noted, as well as reproductive problems and changes in the immune system.

Avoiding exposure:

Avoid contact with car cleaning products. PCBs can be avoided by steering your family clear of hazardous waste sites. Follow standard cleanliness practices such as washing hands thoroughly with soap and water. Avoid contact with old fluorescent lighting fixtures and electrical items such as televisions and refrigerators that were manufactured over 30 years ago. Small amounts of PCBs may leak into the environment from these sources when they are used and exposed skin could be contaminated.

Be wary of food such as fish that may come from contaminated areas such as lakes and streams. Meat and dairy products from nearby are also suspect and should be avoided if possible. To be safe, avoid known toxic sites where there could be PCBs in the air and use caution when drinking water from wells near contaminated sites.

If you work near old transformers or in situations where you will be exposed to PCBs at work, it is possible to bring the toxins home on your skin and clothing. As a precaution, it is recommended that you shower and change your clothes before coming home and wash your work clothes separately.

If you are concerned that you might have been exposed to PCBs there are tests available to measure their level in your body. If you show elevated levels, however, there is no way of telling how and when you were exposed unless you can remember.

Gabriela Rosa

- *In 1990, more than 4,000 toddlers under age four were admitted to hospital emergency rooms as a result of household cleaner-related injuries. That same year, three-fourths of the 18,000 pesticide-related hospital emergency room admissions were children.*

- *Over 80 percent of adults and 90 percent of children in the United States have residues of one or more harmful pesticides in their bodies.*

- *Petrochemical cleaning products in the home are easily absorbed into the skin. Once absorbed, the toxins travel to the blood stream and are deposited in the fatty tissues where they may exist indefinitely.*

—"In Harm's Way," a study by
"The Clean Water Fund" and
"Physicians for Social Responsibility"
May 11, 2000

Phthalates or Phthalate Esters

These chemical compounds are called plasticizers. They belong to a group of substances that are added to plastics to make them more flexible. Their most common use is to make the hard plastic called polyvinyl chloride (PVC) into a softer more flexible plastic. They are colourless and odourless liquids that were first manufactured in the 1920s but since the 1950s, when PVC was introduced, have been produced in large quantities. The most common phthalates are those used in the production of foamed PVC for flooring materials. Some of the chemicals in this group are used as solvents in some pesticides and cleaning products. They are frequently an ingredient of such personal care products as nail polishes, creams, perfumes, as well as being found in fishing lures, paint pigments, adhesives, and caulk.

18

The Awful Truth About Cleaning Products and Fertility

Environmental Occurrence:

Phthalates do not occur naturally in the environment, but they can be found in areas where products containing them have been discarded, such as in disposal areas and landfills. They are found in pesticides and some household products and may persist around the home, or in agricultural areas. Run-off from storms and irrigation may carry them into rivers and streams, where they can be found in low quantities.

Health Risks to Adults:

In the past, the risks to adults have been extrapolated from animal studies that showed high levels of exposure could cause hormonal disruption and damage to organs such as the liver, lungs, kidneys and developing testes and some of the chemicals in the group have been banned from production. Although many products containing phthalates continue to be produced and these are best avoided (so be sure to always inquire if you are uncertain).

Measurements of phthalates in a study of men's urine found a correlation with certain body measurements and hormonal controls, such as insulin resistance, that implied an increased risk of developing Type II diabetes when one has elevated levels of phthalates.

Health risks to children and effect on fertility:

Research suggests phthalates are endocrine disruptors and can cause feminisation of the male embryo. Phthalates have been suspected of causing a reduction of secondary sexual characteristics in male babies. Studies of pregnant women exposed to these substances found high levels of phthalates in their urine. Once their babies were born, some correlation was found between phthalates, male babies and below average gender-related measurements. Also, problems with reproductive organs were correlated to higher concentrations of phthalates in the mother's urine.

Avoiding exposure:

You can help reduce your family's exposure to phthalates in several simple ways. Primarily, if you avoid plastic, PVC and PVC products, you will significantly reduce your risk. Many companies offer PVC-free products. Checking the contents of building materials can help you choose PVC-free products. For example, instead of purchasing clear vinyl windows choose a glass or wood window. Selecting floorings such as tiles or natural materials such as cork, bamboo, or hardwood flooring instead of vinyl can help reduce your exposure to phthalates. In the home, a common PVC problem area is the bathroom, but PVC shower curtains and personal care products such as perfumed and scented products can be eliminated. In addition, when cleaning PVC products it is essential to clean with water rather than harsh chemicals which increase the volatility of the compounds. Choose fragrance-free products and a shower curtain made from a more natural material such as cotton.

Packages with the recycling symbol '3' contain PVC, so steer clear. In addition, many toy manufacturers offer phthalate-free toys and baby products. Many large companies have eliminated PVC products from their inventory.

Store your food in glass container or paper bags, avoid anything with a '3' symbol.

"When combined, chemicals are even more dangerous. Deadly fumes result from mixing ammonia with bleach (both found in many household products) creating lethal "mustard gas!"

—United States Government, Environmental Protection Agency

Parabens

Parabens are chemicals that are used as preservatives in cosmetics and pharmaceuticals and antibacterial products. Their unique bacterial and fungicidal properties make them a popular choice for use in such personal care products as shampoos, moisturisers, gels for shaving and cleansing, toothpastes, topical medications and cleaning products. Common parabens such as butylparaben, ethylparaben, methylparaben and propylparaben are listed on thousands of product packages as ingredients, sometimes even in products that claim to be natural or hypoallergenic. They are both preservatives and food additives, so they are very common in our environment.

Environmental Occurrence:

Parabens that act as antimicrobial agents are often naturally occurring and can be found in plants such as blueberries. Besides their natural presence in some plants, use of parabens in the home and outdoors means that they end up in soil and water and can accumulate in the environment, where their oestrogen mimicking properties have linked them to hormonal disruption in animals.

Health Risks to Adults:

Parabens are one of the main types of EDCs. When products containing parabens are applied to the skin, they can be absorbed by the body and due to their chemical similarity to oestrogen are considered to disrupt hormonal controls. Parabens have been linked to hormonal problems such as weight gain, fluid retention and depression, which are all oestrogen related problems in females. Parabens have also been linked to male reproductive abnormalities. Recent studies show a strong connection to breast cancer.

Gabriela Rosa

Health risks to children and affect on fertility:

The primary risk to fertility occurs because of paraben's oestrogen mimicking chemistry. They have been related to such hormonal disorders as breast cancer, abnormal foetal development and male reproductive abnormalities. The most recent studies have found parabens present in breast cancer tumours. Thus, long-term application of paraben-containing products (such as deodorants, antiperspirants, creams and sprays) by women is potentially harmful. When parabens are applies to the underarms they cause concern as they are in such close proximity to breast tissue, but may also negatively impact fertility. An increased risk of breast cancer due to use of these products has been suggested for many years.

Parabens can be absorbed by the digestive system, the blood stream and the skin and deposited in the body where they can accumulate in breast and other fatty tissue. When ingested, they lose some of their properties, making them less likely to cause problems. It is still not known how long they remain in the body, or what other effects they may have on women's health. In addition because they have a tendency to bio-accumulate in fatty tissues, for men testosterone balance may be a problem with negative affect for fertility and prostate health.

Avoiding exposure:

As awareness is raised about the link between parabens and breast cancer, more companies are producing paraben-free products. These are the products to buy whenever possible. Also choosing fresh and preservative free foods will help eliminate parabens from your diet.

The Awful Truth About Cleaning Products and Fertility

"Of the chemicals found in personal care products:

- *884 are toxic;*

- *146 cause tumors;*

- *218 cause reproductive complications;*

- *778 cause acute toxicity;*

- *314 cause biological mutations;*

- *376 cause skin and eye irritations."*

—United States House of Representatives Report, 1989

Gabriela Rosa

The Truth About Commercial Cleaning Products

Gabriela Rosa

The Truth About Commercial Cleaning Products

THE DAMAGE TO YOUR HOME

Commercial cleaning products are often so harsh they not only damage your health and fertility but often also end up destroying the very things they are supposed to clean. For instance, carpet cleaners often leave carpets frayed and discoloured. To make matters worse, the next morning you wake to find that the stain has reappeared!

Bathroom cleaners with a high acid content can corrode and pit surfaces, creating a perfect hiding place for bacteria and dirt generally creating stains and damage which are impossible to remove or repair.

You want your kitchen to be the cleanest room in your house, because it is the heart of your home. Often the cleaners we use to keep our kitchen sparkling are amongst the most dangerous. Kitchen sponges are known for the huge volumes of bacteria they can harbour (up to 7 billion species)—however you body is apt to deal with these if it needs to however, did you know that the disinfectant you use to clean your sink and counters can leave a harmful toxic residue your body cannot breakdown? Is your kitchen really clean if it is covered in toxins?

INCONSISTENT PRODUCT LABELLING

You can't count on product labels to tell you what chemicals are in a product. The content lists are often incomplete, misleading, and in some cases inaccurate. This leads you to believe that they are safer than they really are. You are not given enough information to make up your own mind and are completely reliant on what the manufacturer has condescended to tell you about the toxic contents of their products.

Becoming Aware Of The Chemical Dangers Around Us

Below is a basic list of dangerous chemicals, which negatively affect your general health and fertility as well as increase your risk of miscarriages. These chemicals are best avoided and ideally should be completely replaced by natural cleaning ingredients:

- Alcohol

- Ammonia

- Bleach

- Butyl cellosolve

- Cresol

- Dye

- Ethanol

- Formaldehyde

- Glycols

- Hydrochloric arid

- Hydrofluoric acid

- Lye

- Naphthalene

- Paradichlorobenzenes (PDCBs)

- Perchloroethylene

- Petroleum distillates

- Phenol

- Phosphoric acid

- Propellants

- Sulphuric acid

- Trichloroethylene (TCE)

Alcohol

Alcohol is a very common ingredient in cleaners and many different kinds are used in commercial cleaners. The following three are the most common:

Ethanol

Commonly used as an ingredient in disinfectants, metal polishes, air fresheners, and degreasers.

The symptoms caused by ingesting large amounts of ethanol can include vomiting, coma, nausea, and death. It is also extremely flammable.

Isopropanol or Isopropyl Alcohol

Isopropanol or Isopropyl are alcohols made from petroleum. As little as 28 grams can be fatal if ingested by a small child. Ingesting or breathing fumes in large quantities can cause dizziness, nausea, vomiting, headaches, depression, or comas. Exposure to high levels of alcohol increases the risk of throat and sinus cancers.

Methanol

Methanol can be found in paint removers, cements, varnishes, and windscreen washing solutions.

Swallowing methanol can cause blurred vision, headaches, inebriation, stomach pain, weakness, blindness, or death.

Ammonia

Ammonia is one of the most common chemicals found in everyday household cleaners. It is used as an ingredient in general-purpose cleaners, glass cleaners, floor cleaners, furniture and metal polishes, oven and toilet bowl cleansers, and in general kitchen cleansers.

The symptoms caused by breathing concentrated ammonia can include irritation to your respiratory system, burning in your eyes and nose, rashes, redness, and even chemical burns. It is not only a hazardous chemical toxin, but when combined with bleach, releases dangerous chloramine gas, which can damage your health and fertility.

Bleach

(Chlorine Bleach or Sodium Hypochlorite)

The first agent of chemical warfare, chlorine, contains highly toxic volatile organic compounds. It was used in both world wars to kill the enemy by asphyxiation and when WWII ended, there was an abundance of this cheap chemical. Then, in the name of huge profits, it was added to our water supply, cleaning products, plastics, pesticides and more. There are definite links between chlorine and cancers of the reproductive system, infertility and miscarriages. In labs, scientists will not handle chlorine without special protective equipment including gloves, facemasks, and ventilation. However, it is in most store-bought cleaning products, including dishwasher detergents. The harmful effects are intensified when the fumes are heated, such as in the shower or when cleaning with hot water. Bleach is commonly present in disinfectants, laundry bleaches, bathroom products, all-purpose cleansers, bath and tile cleaners, and many others—and most women don't even wear gloves when using it!

On top of it all, when bleach is mixed with ammonia it can create a toxic gas called chloramine. The University of Massachusetts Environmental Health and Safety Winter 1999 Newsletter says, 'The inhalation of the noxious fumes associated with the mixing of household cleaners can lead to pulmonary irritation and pneumonitis. Household ammonia... and bleach... are two of the most common cleaning agents. Combining those releases chloramine gas... Typically exposures to low concentrations of chloramines produce only mild respiratory tract irritation. In higher concentrations... may cause corrosive effects and cellular injury, resulting in pneumonitis and oedema." In addition, chlorine affects thyroid function, decreasing fertility and increasing the risk of miscarriages.

Bleach and ammonia are two cleaning solutions that almost every household owns—despite being endocrine disruptors, which damage your health and fertility. They may even be sitting under your sink together. Each is an ingredient in many common cleaners; would you be aware if you unwittingly mixed them?

2-Butoxyethanol

Commonly used in heavy-duty degreasers, window cleaners, all-purpose cleaners, and many others. 2-Butoxyethanol can be absorbed by way of osmosis into the bloodstream. Once absorbed by the skin its effects can include kidney failure as well as damage to the central nervous system, liver, and blood.

Cresol

Though this is a well-known toxic chemical and manufacturers have been reducing its use, it can still be found in a few herbicides, detergents and disinfectants.

Cresol is extremely caustic. Contact with this chemical can cause prickly or severe burning sensations with an ensuing numbness, depression, hyperactivity, and irritability. Indications of chronic poisoning can include loss of appetite, diarrhoea, vomiting, headaches, dizziness, and fatigue. It can also cause allergic reactions resulting in rashes.

Formaldehyde

This chemical is used in detergents, water softeners, and furniture polishes. Items such as mattresses, foam, plastics, plywood, panelling, pressboard, and others, emit formaldehyde as a common pollutant into the air.

Side effects of exposure to high concentrations in the air can include red or watery eyes, respiratory irritation, nausea, and headaches. If ingested in concentrated form formaldehyde can cause stomach pain, coma, bleeding, and even death.

Glycols

Glycols are used in degreasers, dry cleaning chemicals, floor cleaners, paints, and dyes.

Glycols vary in toxicity. Side effects can range anywhere from mild irritation to eyes, skin, and the respiratory system, to nausea, tremors, kidney damage, liver damage, and reproductive and central nervous system damage. Glycol can evaporate into the air adding to the pollutants in your home. When inhaled they can be absorbed through the lungs and skin into the bloodstream.

Hydrochloric Acid

Hydrochloric acid can be found in bathroom cleaning products, lime removers, and metal polishes.

Hydrochloric acid was discovered around the year 800 by alchemist Jabir ibn Hayyan. It holds a place in myths and legends as mediaeval alchemists used it in their quest for the philosopher's stone. It is also an extremely caustic chemical. If it comes in direct contact with your skin it can cause burns, permanent scarring, blindness, and can actually dissolve delicate tissue. Breathing in the vapours from this chemical can cause irritation to your eyes, nose, and throat. Vapours can even cause wheezing or suffocation.

Hydrofluoric Acid

It can be found in aluminium cleaners and rust removers.

Hydrofluoric acid is extremely toxic and caustic. It should be handled with tremendous care, more than that given to other mineral acids such as hydrochloric or sulphuric.

The effects of exposure to skin of diluted hydrofluoric acid are often instantly felt. Exposure to as little as 10% of the body can result in death, even after medical treatment. Exposure to highly concentrated solutions of hydrofluoric acid may even lead to severe hypocalcaemia and death. If as little as 2% of your body is exposed, it can be fatal. For most people this represents no more than the palm of your hand or the sole of your foot.

Exposure can also result in sometimes fatal liver damage, kidney damage, or heart and nerve damage.

Sodium Hydroxide (Lye)

Lye is commonly used as an ingredient in bathroom cleaners, oven cleaners, and drain cleaners. Drain cleaners often contain very concentrated solutions of sodium hydroxide.

If you are familiar with popular crime dramas, you probably know the more gruesome uses for sodium hydroxide. It is also used as a chemical weapon. Should we really be cleaning our homes with a substance so toxic it can be used in chemical warfare?

Sodium hydroxide can also be used to decompose bodies. If it is ingested it will literally eat from the inside out, dissolving the oesophagus, eyes, skin, and face. A little as one drop can be fatal.

Naphthalene

Naphthalene can be found in carpet cleaners, bathroom cleaners, air fresheners, and mothballs.

Naphthalene is particularly dangerous to young children and infants. Exposure to high quantities of naphthalene may harm and destroy red blood cells, which can lead to fatigue, pallor, loss of appetite, restlessness, and may also cause nausea, diarrhoea, vomiting, jaundice, and blood in the urine. It has also been implicated as a possible carcinogen.

Some of the most acute cases of toxic exposure come from infants wearing clothes that have been stored in mothballs.

P-Dichlorobenzene (p-DCB)

This is an ingredient found in mothballs, insecticides, room deodorisers, and toilet fresheners. Exposure to high concentrations of p-DCB can cause headaches, dizziness, and liver problems. The US Department of Health and Human Services has established that p-DCB is a possible carcinogen. Employees who are exposed to extreme concentrations of p-DBC complain of painful irritation in the eyes and nose.

Tetrachloroethylene

This chemical is an ingredient found in dry cleaning liquid and stain removers.

Breathing in vapours from tetrachloroethylene can result in headaches, dizziness, confusion, nausea, sleepiness, unconsciousness, difficulty walking and speaking, and death. Workers who have excessive contact with tetrachloroethylene to their skin may have acute skin irritation, due to fats in the skin being dissolved.

Hydrocarbons (Petroleum Distillates)

They are often ingredients in furniture and metal polishes, pesticides, and oven cleaners.

Hydrocarbons are derived from petroleum and consist mostly of hydrogen and carbon. There are many types of hydrocarbons, with a range of toxicities. Although one well-known hydrocarbon, petroleum jelly, is usually considered to be non-toxic it will definitely negatively impact your fertility. In addition, hydrocarbons such as xylene, benzene, naphthalene, and toluene are very hazardous, and can be dangerous or even fatal if ingested. Symptoms can include chemical pneumonia, temporary nerve-ending desensitisation, skin irritation, and death.

Phenol

Phenols are a possible ingredient in mould and mildew cleaners, disinfectants, air fresheners, and furniture polishes.

Phenol is also known under the older name carbolic acid. It was originally used at the turn of the twentieth century as an antiseptic during surgery. However, it was quickly replaced because of its irritating affects on skin. If phenol comes in contact with the skin it may cause severe chemical burns, swelling, peeling, or hives.

If it is ingested it may cause coma, convulsions, cold sweats or death—as little as 2% in a solution can have dangerous effects on your health such as burning, numbness, or gangrene.

Propellants (Propane, Butane, and less often CFCs)

Propellants are used in aerosol products, furniture polishes, insecticides, and air fresheners.

Normally we can see or smell what we are being exposed to, recognise it, and in the case of toxic chemicals, avoid it. What makes propellants dangerous? In most cases you cannot see them, smell them, and you probably won't even realise they are there. All you have to do is breathe to expose yourself to these harmful chemicals, and their effects on your health are real. They are easily absorbed into the bloodstream through your lungs and can even cause death.

Sulphuric Acid

This is an ingredient in bathroom cleaners and metal polishes. Sulphuric acid is a known constituent of acid rain. If sulphuric acid touches your skin it can be incredibly damaging. Contact can case acute chemical burns, scarring, and blindness; even diluted it can cause severe damage.

Trichloroethylene (TCE)

Trichloroethylene can be found in some stain removers and metal polishes. While its use is being phased out it can still be found in some commercial products.

Breathing the vapours from trichloroethylene may cause headaches, confusion, dizziness, or with prolonged exposure lead to coma. In very high concentrations it can even cause death. Be careful wherever you suspect a high concentration of trichloroethylene vapour, as your nose can become desensitised to its odour and you may unwittingly inhale dangerous or fatal amounts.

Xylene

Xylene can be found in degreasers and it is a petroleum derivative. It is one of the top thirty chemicals currently in use in domestic products. So, it must be pretty safe, right?

Well, you can decide for yourself. Studies have indicated that exposure to high concentrations of xylene can affect the way our brain works, causing lack of muscle coordination, confusion, dizziness, and loss of balance. Milder exposure can result in irritation to the eyes, nose, throat, and skin, lung difficulties, memory problems, and trouble breathing. In very high concentrations it can be fatal. Studies involving unborn animals indicated a high risk of impaired growth and development and even death. The mothers who were also exposed showed similar signs of damage.

The Awful Truth About Cleaning Products and Fertility

Chemical Name	Health Impact	Commonly Contained In
2-Butoxyethanol	Liver and kidney damage Neurotoxin	All-purpose cleaners Window cleaners Spray cleaners Scouring powders
Akanol amines	Carcinogen [precursors]	All-purpose cleaners
Alkyl phenoxy ethanols	Hormone disruptor	Laundry detergents All-purpose cleaners
Amyl acetate	Neurotoxin	Furniture polishes
Cresol	Liver and kidney damage Neurotoxin	Disinfectants
Crystalline silica	Carcinogen	All-purpose cleaners Scouring powders
Dichloroisocyanurate	Reproductive and immune system development disruptor	Tub and tile cleaners Scouring powders Dishwasher powders
Diethanolamines	Carcinogenic [nitrosamines]	All-purpose cleaners Detergents Dishwashing liquids
Dioxane	Immunosuppressant Carcinogen	Window cleaners Laundry liquids Dishwashing liquids
Ethylene glycol	Neurotoxin	All-purpose cleaners
Formaldehyde	Carcinogen	Deodorisers Disinfectants Germicides

Glycol ethers	Reproductive system toxin Liver and kidney damage Neurotoxin	All-purpose cleaners Window cleaners Spray cleaners Scouring powders
Hydrocarbons	Lungs	Furniture/metal polishes Oven cleaners Pesticides
Hydrochloric Acid	Skin [solvent, irritant] Respiratory system	Lime removers Metal polishes Bathroom cleaners
Hydrofluoric acid	Liver and kidneys Heart Nerves	Aluminium cleaners Rust removers
Methanol	Central Nervous System Liver [toxin]	Paint Removers Windscreen washer fluids Varnishes Inks
Methylene chloride	Carcinogen Liver/Kidney Neurotoxin Cardiac [trigger]	Degreasers
Morpholine	Liver and kidney [toxin]	All-purpose cleaners Waxes Polishes
Naphthalene	Kidney [toxin] Cataracts [trigger] Carcinogen	Carpet cleaners Deodorisers Toilet cleaners
Nitrobenzene	Blood [poison]	Polishes

The Awful Truth About Cleaning Products and Fertility

P-dichlorobenzene	Hormone disruptor Carcinogen	Deodorisers Mothballs
Phenol	General [poison]	Mould and mildew cleaners Polishes
Phosphoric acid	Skin [toxin]	Tub and tile cleaners Toilet cleaners
Propylene Glycol [Anti-freeze]	Kidney and liver [damage] Eyes and skin [irritant]	Toothpaste Body lotions Cosmetics Deodorants Hair conditioners Skin creams
Sodium hydroxide [Lye]	Skin [chemical burns] Eyes [blindness]	Drain cleaners
Sodium hypochlorite [Bleach]	Irritant Carcinogen [precursor]	Bleaches Scouring powder Toilet bowl cleaners Disinfectants
Sodium Laurel Sulphate	Skin Hair Tissues	Bubble baths Shampoos Shower gels Engine degreasers Garage floor cleaners
Stoddard Solvent	Neurotoxin	Degreasers Stain removers

Sulphuric Acid	Skin [burns]	Bathroom cleaners Metal polishes
Tetrachloroethylene	Central Nervous System [depressant]	Dry cleaning liquids Stain removers
Xylene	Reproductive system Kidneys Development [toxin]	Degreasers

WHY SWITCH TO NATURAL CLEANING METHODS?

Their attractive labels beckon to us, luring us to buy with pictures of breezy spring meadows and cool waterfalls. They seem to be saying to us, if we buy these cleaners our homes will be clean and healthy places for us and our families to live; but under their tempting veneers are hazardous toxic chemicals.

Open your cleaning cupboard and what do you see? Products you have used for years, items you not only trust and expect to be safe, but ones your mother, and possibly grandmother, used and trusted too. They are familiar, and they are convenient; but they are dangerous. What you are really looking at is a toxic waste site. Many of the chemicals in those innocent looking bottles are surprisingly hazardous. Some, such as those found in drain cleaners, not only clear clogged drains – they also dissolve your skin and ruin your fertility—but they are not alone. The vast majority of cleaning products you buy from the supermarket perform in a very similar way.

The list of chemicals approved for use in cleaning products is very small, and the availability of comprehensive data on the way these chemicals impact on our health is limited. Ninety per cent of registered chemicals have incomplete data on their effects on human health. We only find out about the damage caused by these toxic chemicals once an innocent person has been harmed. In other words, we are guinea pigs for commercial profit.

For the sake of your health and fertility—changes in this area are paramount. Avoiding toxic chemicals in conventional cleaning products is essential—even if you have a cleaner and do not come into direct contact with products, if they are being used in your home and office environments you will eventually be in contact and affected by the fumes and/or residues. So train your cleaner to use your new, natural products and system or find another one that will—your health is too important.

Other Important Precautions When Cleaning!

The chemicals used to clean are only one small part of the danger of what you can be exposed to during the process. It is key when cleaning to guard yourself by wearing protective clothing and equipment where necessary. Particularly when cleaning dusty environments such as roofs, garages and other polluted spaces because in the settled dust or grime are often found extremely toxic substances such as asbestos, fumes, chemicals, heavy metals and other noxious pollutants that will negatively affect your health and fertility.

Always wear a mask covering your nose and mouth even when doing household cleaning of particularly dusty or long-term closed off areas. When cleaning, if you know you are likely to be in contact with dangerous substances the use of protective goggles are also in order. In addition, it is essential that when you do such dirty work you wear long pants and long sleeved shirts to prevent toxic absorption through the skin. As soon as you finish the task, either dispose of or thoroughly wash the clothes you were wearing and have a long shower to clean yourself.

If you and your partner are trying to conceive or are preparing for a conception attempt, the ideal option is to delegate 'heavy cleaning' tasks to a third party if possible.

DO NATURAL METHODS WORK?

The answer is a pure and natural "yes". In some instances they may not be as immediately effective as their toxic counterparts, and they may require a little longer soaking or scrubbing, but they are infinitely safer for your health, your family, and your home.

This book gives you all the knowledge and tools you need to make your own natural products, but it also give you information about other natural cleaning systems that you may find useful if you decide you want to buy natural products instead of making them yourself. Either way, some of the recipes in this book have been used for hundreds or thousands of years. They are tried and true and have kept everything from the grandest mansion to the most humble cottage clean and healthy using simple, natural and inexpensive ingredients. Remember that it has only been recently that we as a society have ventured onto the path of chemical cleaning.

In this short period, we have, however, had enough time to study the effects of toxic chemicals on our health and those of our children and loved ones, so how can we consider using anything other than natural methods to clean our homes? Creating our own natural cleaners will make a safer, healthier environment for us, our families and future generations.

OH WHAT A SAVING!

Another great advantage of making your own natural products (besides safeguarding you and your family's health) is that they will save you money. Natural products may often cost only cents compared to the many dollars similar commercial chemical cleaners can cost dollars or more.

Most of us do not realise how much we spend on toxic household cleaners. We pick up a general purpose kitchen cleaner, a tub and tile cleaner, a disinfectant, place them in our shopping trolleys and are on our way without once thinking of the cost. After all, they are products we use every day, and we would not think twice about buying a litre of milk or a loaf of bread, but a few simple cleaners in our shopping trolley can add up thousands of dollars per year. And what about the environmental damage and impact caused? And the legacy our choices leave the generations that follow? What's the price of that?

The cost of making the same non-toxic products using natural ingredients, with the peace of mind that comes from knowing exactly what you are being exposed to, is around $5.50 a month!

You may be tempted to throw out your old toxic cleaners or pour them down the drain to begin afresh using the recipes contained in this book, but please refrain. Your local council has systems in place for disposing of toxic chemicals, and yes, your everyday household products are considered hazardous material, so placing full bottles of cleaning products in your regular garbage is often illegal. Call your local waste management department for suggestions and assistance in disposing of your old chemical cleaners. When you do this, also remember that you will be doing the air in your home a favour, because you may think just because these products are 'safely' stored in your cupboard they are not doing damage. Think again, they still outgas in storage and affect your health even when you least expect it.

WHAT IS THE TRUE MEANING OF NON-TOXIC?

Bicarbonate soda, salt, vinegar, lemon and lime juice, soda water and other natural cleaning ingredients are often referred to as 'non-toxic', but what does that really mean?

Non-toxic cleaning products do not pose the risks to health and fertility normally associated with traditional toxic cleaners. Generally, as a rule of thumb, if you can eat it, you can clean with it. It does not mean you will, especially since in excessive dosages most things are dangerous. Using non-toxic cleaners does not mean you can carelessly eat them, pour them into your eyes, squirt them all over your skin, or be careless with it. However it does mean that if an accident occurs while you are using them and some spills on you, it does not mean a trip to the doctor or hospital and your family's health and fertility are not compromised in the long run.

Beginning With
The Basics

Beginning With The Basics

Now that you are ready to begin cleaning naturally, let's look at the ingredients used for creating our own, safe, natural products.

You probably already have most of the basic ingredients, such as white distilled vinegar or bicarbonate of soda, so you can begin making some recipes right away.

INGREDIENTS

Derivatives and Extracts from Plants

GRAPEFRUIT SEED EXTRACT

Where to buy:

Heath food stores.

About:

The liquid extract of grapefruit seeds. It is a powerful antibacterial agent.

WHITE DISTILLED VINEGAR

Where to buy:

Salad dressing aisle of the supermarket, or at discount stores, and bulk supply houses. You definitely want to buy the natural, edible version, not the 'cleaning' version.

About:

Be sure to buy white vinegar not any other variety (e.g. apple cider vinegar) to use in cleaning recipes as it can stain some surfaces. Buy a good brand of vinegar made from grains, not petroleum derivatives.

If you buy a few litres of vinegar you should be set for a while because vinegar is one of the main ingredients in the following home-cleaning recipes. Vinegar has a very long shelf life, it does not spoil easily. If you want to test a few recipes first, you can buy smaller bottles. Because the small bottles are usually made from glass they can be saved and recycled as storage bottles for other home products.

Vinegar is an acid and works very well for removing soap scum, mineral deposits and odours, because it neutralises alkaline material.

LIQUID CASTILE SOAP (VEGETABLE OIL OR GLYCERINE-BASED)

Where to buy:

Health food stores or in the health food section of your supermarket, and also through mail order companies or online.

About:

Most of these soaps are concentrated. Liquid castile soap is the main ingredient of many of the recipes in this book so feel free to buy a large size. You will want to use it frequently, so you will probably run out quickly.

Liquid soap is a great dirt buster because it removes dirt stuck on surfaces and objects by dissolving the oils that bind the dirt.

ESSENTIAL OILS

Where to buy:

Health food stores, chemists, online and mail order companies.

About:

There are many types of essential oils. Essential oils are distilled from flowers, roots, trees, leaves, fruits, and grasses. There are literally hundreds of essential oils and they are used for everything from essential oil burners to aromatherapy massages, and home-made cleaning products as well as natural air fresheners to insect repellents. They are really versatile.

Be sure to only buy 100% pure essential oils. Although these are more expensive, they last longer and are of higher quality. Most diluted essential oils are of poorer quality and are diluted in cheap base vegetable oils. These are not suitable for your cleaning formulae.

Warning:

If you are pregnant avoid using the essential oils of basil, cedar wood, chamomile, clary sage, geranium, jasmine, juniper, peppermint, rose, rosemary, myrrh, sage, wintergreen, thyme, and pennyroyal.

Generally, also be aware that 100% pure essential oils are highly concentrated so be careful when using them. It is always advisable to wear protective gloves when handling them as certain oils can burn the skin when undiluted. Never drink essential oils or any solutions containing them, no matter how good they smell, and also be careful to avoid contact with your eyes.

If you have never bought essential oils before, here is a starter kit for you to consider. These essential oils are ones you will want to have on hand when making recipes. Feel free to add to this list too as you become familiar with the scents you prefer! There are so many wonderful (natural and non-toxic) fragrances you will want to buy definitely experiment with them and you will soon discover your favourites. It is like a whole new world of possibilities will open up for you.

Essential Oil Of	Special Note
Citronella	Great as an insect repellent!
Citrus	Lemon, Sweet Orange, Lime, or all three Find out properties
Tea-tree	An Australian favourite. A great antimicrobial and antiseptic.
Wintergreen	Handle with caution—find out how toxic it is and what properties it has.

Other essential oils you will want to keep on hand

Basil
Lavender
Lemon Balm
Mint
Oregano
Rosemary
Sage
Thyme

A list of the essential oils most commonly used for the recipes in this book.

Cedar

Citronella

Eucalyptus

Lavender

Lemon

Lime

Mint (peppermint, wintergreen, spearmint)

Pine

Rosemary

Sweet orange

Can You Make Your Own Essential Oils?

Absolutely! Although this is not as easy as it may sound and you do need special equipment.

The highest quality essential oils are often made by steam distillation and it can be a fun and rewarding hobby, especially when you grow your own herbs. Personally I find it easier to buy them. However you may discover a brand new love affair or even a little side business for yourself in the process.

There are many different kinds of home stills for purchase. You can find them through herbal or essential oil supply companies. A good starter home distiller can be purchased for around fifty dollars.

Which Essential Oils Should I Choose?

Throughout the recipes in this book I recommend blends of essential oils and herbs to use. However, I encourage you to try making your own substitutions whenever they are suggested in the recipes. Use the following table of essential oils and their uses to aid you in making substitutions. This is a list of popular herbs/oils that you can easily buy from most essential oil stockist.

Essential Oil	Properties
Basil**	Antiseptic, antibacterial
Bay	Antibacterial
Bergamot*	Antibiotic
Camphor	Antibacterial
Cardamom	Antibacterial
Cedar wood**	Antiseptic, antifungal
Chamomile**	Antibiotic, antibacterial
Cinnamon	Antiviral
Citronella	Antibacterial
Clary sage**	Antiseptic, deodorant
Clove	Antibiotic, antiviral
Cypress	Antibacterial
Eucalyptus	Antibiotic, antifungal, antiviral, antibacterial
Frankincense	Antiseptic

Geranium**	Antiseptic, deodorant
Ginger	Antibacterial
Grapefruit*	Antiseptic, disinfectant
Hyssop	Antibiotic, antibacterial
Jasmine**	Antiseptic
Juniper**	Antifungal, antibacterial
Lavender	Antibiotic, antifungal, antiviral, antibacterial
Lemon*	Antibiotic, antifungal, antiviral, antibacterial
Lemongrass	Antibacterial
Lemon verbena	Antibacterial
Lime*	Antibiotic, antibacterial
Marjoram	Antibacterial
Myrtle	Antibiotic, antifungal
Neroli	Antiseptic, antibacterial, deodorant
Nutmeg	Antibiotic
Orange*	Antibacterial
Oregano	Antibiotic, antiviral
Palmarosa	Antiseptic, antiviral, antibacterial
Patchouli	Antibiotic, antifungal
Peppermint**	Antiseptic

Pine	Antibiotic, antibacterial
Rose**	Antiseptic
Rosemary**	Antibacterial
Rosewood	Antiseptic, antibacterial, deodorant
Sage**	Antifungal, antibacterial
Sandalwood	Antifungal, antiviral, antibacterial
Savory	Antifungal
Spearmint	Antibacterial
Tea-tree	Antibiotic, antifungal, antiviral, antibacterial
Thyme**	Antibacterial, antifungal, antiviral, antibacterial
Verbena (aka vervain)	Antibacterial
Wintergreen* **	Antibacterial
Ylang ylang	Antiseptic

*Exercise caution when handling these essential oils. Wearing protective gloves is recommended.

**Avoid using if you are pregnant.

ADDITIONAL OILS

When buying oils, as in the case of essential oils be sure they are 100% pure. Avoid any oils that are mixed or have 'mineral oil' as an ingredient, as this is petroleum based.

ALMOND OIL

Where to buy:

Health food stores, some supermarkets and chemists.

About:

The oil extracted from the almond nut, is a rich moisturising oil also used for lubrication.

APRICOT KERNEL OIL (AKA PERSIC OIL)

Where to buy:

Health food stores.

About:

This is a natural oil derived from the kernel of an apricot, and known for its moisturising and lubricating properties. It can even be used a body and face moisturiser.

CARNAUBA WAX

Where to buy:

Health food stores, online, or through select mail order companies and furniture stores.

About:

Carnauba wax is also called the 'queen of waxes' and is made from the leaves of the carnauba palm, a native of north-eastern Brazil. It is the hardest natural wax.

COCOA BUTTER

Where to buy:

Health food stores, online, or through select mail order companies.

About:

Cocoa butter is extracted from the cacao bean during the chocolate making process and it works well as a stabilising agent in creams.

COCONUT OIL

Where to buy:

Health food stores, some chemists, and through mail order companies.

About:

Also known as coconut butter, coconut oil is extracted from the insides of coconuts. It has a smooth buttery texture and is excellent for use in soaps because it lathers well, and works as a stabiliser in mixtures. It does not stain and is easy to rinse off.

JOJOBA OIL

Where to buy:

Health food stores and herbal suppliers.

About:

Jojoba oil is a unique liquid wax made from the seeds of the jojoba shrub, a native of Mexico and the south-western United States. It is said to have antiseptic properties and is an excellent lubricant. It never spoils. It is very light, extremely nourishing and readily absorbed by the skin. It is also a great body and face moisturiser.

LINSEED OIL (FLAX SEED OIL)

Where to buy:

Health food stores.

Special note on shopping for linseed oil:

The linseed oil found in hardware stores usually contains chemical drying agents and should be avoided. You want to buy the edible type.

About:

Linseed oil is extracted from the dried seeds of flax. It has many uses for naturally finishing and polishing wood. Linseed oil will harden when exposed to the air.

WALNUT OIL

Where to buy:

Health food stores and some chemists.

About:

Walnut oil is extracted from the flesh of walnuts. In addition to its use in cleaning recipes walnut oils is another possible face and body moisturiser.

MINERALS

BICARBONATE OF SODA

Where to buy:

This can be found in the baking aisle of supermarkets, discount stores, chemists, and bulk supply houses.

About:

There are many brands of bicarbonate of soda available. You will probably want to buy several boxes of bicarbonate of soda as it is a main ingredient in many of the natural cleaning recipes. Like vinegar, bicarbonate of soda has a very long shelf life.

Gabriela Rosa

Speed Cleaning

Fast Track Your Clean

TOOLS OF THE TRADE

There have been many changes in our society since our ancestors maintained their homes and were able to devote a significant portion of their day to this task. Nowadays we are faced with such an array of demands on our time that there is very little left for leisure and almost none for daily chores such as house cleaning. Besides who wants to spend more time than absolutely necessary cleaning, anyway?

That being said, there is one thing that has remained constant through the intervening years–the dirt.

Unless you consider cleaning your home a leisure activity, this guide is as much about personal freedom as it is about cleaning.

This guide gives you the knowledge you need to be a tradesman when it comes to house cleaning. It applies well-known commercial cleaning techniques, based on time and motion studies, to the process of cleaning your home. These techniques will reduce the time you spend cleaning by at least 50%. All the successful commercial maintenance services know and use these techniques, and so can you .

The first step is to obtain your tools and supplies. There are specific recipes in this book for excellent cleaning solutions. Start by choosing and creating your solutions. Place these in appropriate spray-type bottles, squeeze bottles or other containers. Now you will need your tools.

Tools and Supplies

As mentioned, cleaning should be approached as a trade. As with any trade you will need tools. Some you may already have otherwise you may need to get them. Having the right tools will speed up the process optimising your time and allowing you to do a job you will be proud to call yours!

Once you are properly equipped it is important to maintain your tools and supplies. Do not sabotage your own best efforts by letting your tools wear out and your supplies run low. Make certain you replace them as needed.

The next step is to put your equipment in the correct places. If left lying around the house you will waste valuable time. You don't want to spend as much time collecting your tools and supplies as you take you to do your cleaning! You will find out where best to store each item in the related chapter, but be warned you will need a cleaning apron to keep it all in order.

Cleaning Apron

Your cleaning apron is the most important part of the process. Remember, this is about natural, healthy cleaning in minimal time, with little effort—not a fashion parade. The apron you choose should have a number of pockets of different sizes. It should also have some loops on which you can easily hang things. You will need to wear your apron every time you clean. It will dramatically improve your efficiency and will save you loads of time because you will have everything on hand exactly when you need it.

Three of the pockets will be used exclusively for the following tools:

Toothbrush

No, not for brushing your teeth! It is for getting into small places such as in between tiles, where the tap meets the sink, light switches, nooks and crannies on stove tops etc. Often when you wipe something a residue will be left which will just not come off. Using the toothbrush and your Red Liquid* cleaner will remove it. A toothbrush you are finished with will do, but it may need to be replaced regularly, as the bristle become very worn and spread apart.

*Explained in more detail later.

Razor-blade scraper

This is indispensable when removing stubborn grime from glass, porcelain or other hard smooth surfaces. It could be soap film in the bathroom, paint drops on glass, spots on oven glass or appliances, etc.

Scraper

This is a standard scraper you can find at the paint store, sometimes called a putty knife. It is excellent for those odd blobs that are too stuck to remove with a toothbrush. It should be about four centimetres (one and a half inches) in width.

Trash Pocket

While you may not think of this as a tool, you should take a re-sealable plastic bag and line one of the pockets on your apron. Use paper clips to secure it to the top of the pocket. You will use this as a temporary trash bag for anything odd and possibly nasty you may encounter.

Carry Caddy

This should have a convenient handle for carrying. It will act as permanent storage for your cleaning supplies, keeping everything nice, simple and together for optimum speed.

Bottle of Red Liquid

This is a spray bottle that contains your natural, general spray-and-wipe cleaner for surfaces other than glass. You will also have several smaller spray bottles in your apron or carry caddy, which contain specialised cleaners. In the cleaning instructions where you see a request for Red Liquid you will need to take into consideration what you are cleaning at the time, as you may need to use one of your specialised cleaners on particular surfaces. General purpose recipes are easy to find throughout the book.

Bottle of Blue Liquid

This is a spray bottle containing the cleaner you will use for glass.

The spray bottles should have a squeeze handle which can be hooked into the loops on your apron. They should also have a nozzle that can be adjusted by turning.

Tile Liquid

This is the cleaner you will use to clean your bath, shower and tiles. It will remove soap film and mineral deposits in and around the bath and shower. Keep this cleaner in a spray bottle.

Feather Duster

While it is true that a feather duster only moves dust from one place to another, there are times when this is exactly what you want to achieve.

If you are cleaning for short periods on a regular basis, moving dust from a higher level, which might be difficult to reach, to a lower level, where it can be vacuumed up, is definitely worthwhile. A good feather duster is the best way to accomplish this task.

The best natural feather dusters are made from ostrich down. You should buy one that is about 50 centimetres (18 inches) long, including the handle. They are not cheap, but you get what you pay for, and you will appreciate how well these work.

As far as a completely natural cleaning system technologies go, I am a fan of Enjo. You buy it once and you have it for life. The Enjo all-purpose flexi is the best choice for an all round duster. It has an extension handle so it can reach high areas, such as the tops of bookshelves and ceiling corners.

Cleaning cloths

This is where Enjo's microfibre technology all-purpose cloths excel! They remove dirt and bacteria, leaving surfaces clean and chemical free. With Enjo your Red Liquid can simply be water. It is an investment in your family's health definitely worth considering.

Either way, the best cleaning cloth are microfibre ones. I have been using them for years and would not give them away for anything. I have dozens of them and since they are lint free. It's the best and fastest cleaning experience you will ever have, particularly for glass and mirrors.

Alternatively, if you want to use a plain cloth, it is ideal to buy white pure cotton cloths. These can be found at your local linen service—it enables you to see how dirty a surface or location is throughout your cleaning meaning you know exactly when you can stop. This dramatically speeds up the whole process. If you have been using old T-shirts, underwear, socks, sheets or old newspapers, definitely replace those during your general cleaning, however, do keep rags aside for situations where you would not want to keep your cleaning cloth for future use (e.g. carpet cleaning etc). You need to have enough white cloths on hand not to run out of them while you are cleaning, and they should be replaced when they become too worn for effective use. They should be washed in hot water to sanitise them.

My mum has one (white cotton cloth) clearly marked for the type of cleaning they are intended Her special furniture gets dusted with a very soft, damp cloth, which clean nothing else and therefore does not collect dirt which can scratch delicate surfaces. General dusting gets another clot (or several) and so it goes. She's very organised and of course I've been well trained. Whichever you choose (cotton or microfibre), we will be referring to them as 'cleaning cloths' from now on.

At the end of each cleaning session, do a machine load with tea tree oil (as a sanitizer) and let them all dry in the sun. Once dry, neatly fold all your cleaning clots and place them in your carry caddy for the next cleaning day.

Spray Furniture Polish

Keep whichever recipe you decide to use as furniture polish in a spray bottle. This spray bottle can be smaller than the ones used for your Red and Blue liquids and should fit in a pocket of your apron.

Furniture polishing cloth

Choose a soft cotton or Microfibre cloth for this purpose. Keep in mind it is always a good idea to remove all dust with a damp cloth prior to polishing in order to avoid scratching 'delicate' surfaces. The furniture polishing cloth should only be used for polishing furniture, put a small mark on it for identification. Do not use this with any other cleaner, particularly those that are powder-based. Residue can remain in the cloth and scratch your furniture.

Small plastic container

This can be any small plastic cup-type container, which can be filled with water and used to rinse hard to reach spots.

Whisk Broom

Choose one with plastic bristles. It will be used on your stairs and for general brushing, such as between static cushions on your furniture.

Extension cord, 20 meters(50-foot), with cord caddy

You should buy a rounded extension cord, which is more resistant to tangling. The cord caddy is ideal as it will save you a lot of time in the long run.

Toilet brush

Choose a brush with stiff bristles, which are better for scrubbing. Do not get the ones with the twisted wire.

Tile brush

This is a brush that has about five centimetres (two inches) of stiff synthetic bristles. You will use this brush on the tile and grout in the bathroom. It will also be used for the tub and bathroom sink.

Sponges

Select several sponges of different colours. Choose different colours for different types of cleaning areas. Colour coding your cleaning items will save you lots of time.

Scrub pad/sponge—General

A Microfibre glove or sponge with an interwoven scouring patch is ideal for general cleaning and often works with just water.

However in instances where water simply will not get the job done, you can resort to the trusty bicarbonate soda and vinegar paste. Here's a simple way to use it. Take one pad/sponge, soak in water and wring out. Place bicarbonate of soda on this pad. Soak a second pad in vinegar and wring it out. Layer the two pads, one on top of the other. Place the pad with the bicarbonate of soda onto the surface to be cleaned and as you start to press and clean, the vinegar and bicarbonate of soda will react, creating the cleaning agent. You can also just use a pad soaked with vinegar and put the bicarbonate of soda on this pad or straight onto the surface. Both methods work equally well, and even your great great-grandparents would approve.

Scrub pad/sponge—Oven

This is the same as the one used for general cleaning except you will keep a spare one to use exclusively for the oven.

Mop

Most mops, either sponge or cloth, are satisfactory. Be sure these are washed and cleaned thoroughly after use and put outside to dry properly before storing away. Replace your mop every couple of months (just as you would do with a kitchen sponge).

Personally I don't like or use mops as they tend to shift bacteria around the floor because they are very difficult to clean. I have bought large sized hand towels or small bath towels specifically for floor cleaning. You can wrap them around a large broom and use instead of a mop to clean the floor brilliantly!

I wrap a floor towels around my 'giant floor squeegee', which is similar to a window cleaning squeegee, except it has a normal broom stick attached to it. It's about 50cm wide and it cleans a lot of hard to reach places. The best thing about it is that once I am done with my cleaning. I throw all my cleaning cloths and towels (except for the furniture polishing cloth) into the washing machine for a hot water load with a full cup of vinegar or hydrogen peroxide to ensure my cleaning towels are thoroughly and naturally sanitised.

Oven Cleaner

Once you have mixed up your oven cleaner, keep it in a plastic spray bottle. This should be one of the smaller ones that can fit in a pocket of your apron. The best time to clean the oven is just after use when it's still warm, as the grease is soft and easy to wipe off.

Floor cleaner/Polisher

A smaller spray bottle of your preferred floor cleaner, kept in a pocket of your apron.

Vacuum cleaner

Choose one that you find reliable and convenient to use based on its size. Do not select one that is too large for you to pick up and manoeuvre.

Miscellaneous tools

Keep these tools just for your cleaning. Do not let others in your home take them: pliers, flat-head screwdriver, Phillips head screwdriver, can of compressed air, spare vacuum cleaner bag. If you are using a vacuum that does not require a bag, place a small plastic bag in your carry caddy so that you can empty the vacuum while you are working.

RULES OF THE TRADE

Never Waste Motion

The goal is to be able to walk around the room once and have the cleaning complete, so you must have all the tools and supplies you need with you. You don't want to have to make many needless trips to pick up tools and supplies. Cleaning in a specific order means you do not back track.

Have The Tool You Need

Without your tools, you can never be effective. That includes your apron and your caddy of course!

Always Work From Top To Bottom

That means always. Do not cheat on this one. The absolute only exception is if you are washing walls—see 'hints for walls' section.

Only Clean Something If It Is Dirty

Your time is valuable, so pretend that you are cleaning for money. Prioritise your cleaning; vertical surfaces are never as dirty as horizontal surfaces. Upper surfaces are not as likely to be as dirty as lower surfaces. Often all there will be on a surface are a few fingerprints, so don't clean the whole surface, unless it is required.

Avoid Over Rinsing

As you clean, look through the dirt you have dislodged to determine if you are done. This avoids rinsing just to see if you are finished.

If The Process You Have Chosen To Clean Something Is Not Working, Change Your Process

Be flexible. If you find that what you are doing is just not working, stop. Try something else.

Keep Your Tools In Good Shape

Don't keep using a tool once it is worn out. It will just cost you time and can even damage surfaces.

Always Put Your Tools Back

It is critical that you put your tools back in your apron in the same place every time. You do not want to spend time fumbling through the pockets on your apron looking for a tool. Do not lay the tool down, it will walk off!

Work On The Clock

Clean on the clock. Try to get faster each time you do a task. Remember, the sooner you are finished with the cleaning the more time there is for other (possibly more enjoyable) activities.

Work In Front

Always keep your work directly in front of you. Do not try to work off to the side. You will be more effective and are less likely to strain yourself.

If You Have Help, Work As A Team

Delegating tasks is important for being effective. You will also need tools and supplies for each person in your team.

Each and Every Room...

Gabriela Rosa

The Kitchen

The Kitchen

Put these items in your carry caddy:

- 1 Can of powdered cleanser

- 1 Blue Liquid

- 1 Red Liquid

- 1 Scrub pad/sponge—General

- 1 Scrub pad/sponge—Oven

- 1 Steel wool pad

- 1 Feather duster

- 1 Whisk broom

- 1 Oven cleaner

- 1 Pair of rubber gloves

- 1 Bottle floor cleaner/polisher

- 10 Cleaning cloths (folded)

- 5 Microfibre technology wipes

- 1 mop (alternative preferred—see Mop on page XX)

Put the following in your apron:

- 1 Scraper

- 1 Toothbrush

- 1 Razor-blade scraper

- 2 Plastic bags with clips

Where To Start?

Lean your mop next to the door and place your carry caddy next to the sink. Facing the sink start by working to your right and making one trip around the kitchen; never turning back.

Start looking for consistency—check that all the items are in the correct apron pockets. Make certain that the Red and Blue Liquids are hanging on their appropriate loops. By doing this you will become accustomed to reaching for the products and finding them without thinking. This will save you a lot of time. If you are wearing pants with back pockets, put the feather duster in one back pocket and the whisk broom in the other back pocket. Otherwise they should be placed in your carry caddy. The whisk broom will be used to remove dirt from vents, and from the corners the vacuum cannot reach. Remove the appropriate number of cloths from your carry caddy (you will know how many after a few times).

Take any rubbish bins from the kitchen and place them just outside the kitchen or in the doorway, so that they will not be in the way when cleaning the floor. Pick up any rugs or floor mats and place them outside the kitchen, flat on the floor. They are now ready to be vacuumed.

Remember to work to the right and from top to bottom. In the kitchen it's probably wise to begin with the cupboards. Next to the handles there will probably be fingerprints. These are removed by spraying lightly with the Red Liquid (your general purpose cleaner of choice). As you replace the Red Liquid on its loop, take a cloth with the other hand and wipe the area. As you work, the cloth will become damp. Keep a dry cloth over your shoulder. When your cloth becomes too damp for streak free cleaning, place it in your apron and put a new dry cloth over your shoulder.

Only clean if it is dirty. It there are no fingerprints to clean, then don't clean. Also, do not spray a large area of a cupboard door and clean it.

Working down, the next place to check is the wall between the cupboards and the counter top (only clean if necessary).

Next is the counter top, which should be cleaned every time. Start by picking up the carry caddy, spray and wipe the counter beneath it, and then replace the carry caddy. Work from back to front. Take each object on the counter and move it directly forward just enough that you can clean behind and underneath where the object was. Work to the right to the end of the counter. Before you put the objects back, wipe them off or dust them, whichever is appropriate. Once replaced, clean the rest of the counter.

Drawer fronts are next. The handles here may need cleaning. In tight spots it may be easier to use your toothbrush than a cloth. Use the Red Liquid and once the tight spots are clean, a cloth will probably keep them that way.

As a cloth becomes too wet to use, either put it in the plastic-lined pocket of your apron, or toss it back into your carry caddy.

Remember to put the supplies and tools back in your apron every time. Never leave them on a counter or anywhere else. Even if this seems odd at first, you need to do it anyway. Every tradesman will tell you that it will make you faster and more efficient.

Residual Issues

When you encounter a spot on the counter, such as a dried food splatter, which is not easily removed with your cloth and Red Liquid, you will need to escalate the cleaning method and use the kitchen glove or white pad/sponge. This should be in your apron in one of the pockets lined with a plastic bag. Again, when you have finished using it, replace it in the same plastic-lined pocket. Don't worry if it becomes dirty, it's being used to loosen dirt, not to remove it.

Use Red Liquid and the white pad/sponge to scrub the offending spot, if it's being stubborn, use your scraper to attack it but be careful not to scratch the surface.

Glass and Mirrors

Use the Blue Liquid and a dry cloth for glass and mirrors. You already have them with you, so you don't have to go and find anything. Spray lightly with Blue Liquid and then wipe with a dry cloth until the surface is completely dry. It is important to use a light spray. Using more will not get the glass any cleaner, it will just make your cloth wetter. Remember to replace the Blue Liquid after each use.

Cobwebs

As you work around the kitchen, always moving to your right, check the line where the ceiling meets the wall. This is a favourite place for cobwebs. Use your feather duster to remove these. If you cannot reach the cobwebs with your feather duster, use the extension wand of your vacuum when you do the floor.

Doors

There are three primary places to check on a door. The first is at the top of the door frame for cobwebs. The second place is the door handle and the frame near it, for fingerprints or smudges. The last place to check is near the bottom of the door, where someone may have left marks with their shoes when pushing the door open.

Shelves without Doors

You can just use a feather duster and dust the front of each shelf or, if it's needed, you should clean one shelf each time you clean the kitchen. When you clean a shelf, if possible, move all of the contents of the shelf to one side, and then clean the clear side. Repeat this process and end with the contents back in their original locations. If there are more items than can be moved to one side, take just enough items from the shelf to make it possible and place them on the bench top.

Refrigerator—Exterior

Start at the flat top of the refrigerator. Once you are cleaning the kitchen on a regular basis, you should be able to just feather dust this. If the top of your refrigerator is used as a shelf for storing objects, treat it as a shelf for cleaning.

Clean fingerprints from the front and sides of the refrigerator. Do not clean the entire surface of the refrigerator unless it needs it. There may be a nameplate and also tiny crevices where the handle meets the surface of the refrigerator. Use your toothbrush to clean these areas.

Now open the refrigerator door to clean the door seal. If necessary, use your toothbrush to get it clean.

With the door still open clean the vent at the bottom of the refrigerator. If it is just dusty use your whisk broom, otherwise wipe it clean. Also, with the door open, wipe down the frame of the refrigerator and wipe any obvious dirt from the shelves. Don't get carried away or you will spend all your time cleaning the inside of the refrigerator, which is not what you set out to do at this point. When you need to clean the inside of the fridge, ideally it is good to set a specific time for this task 'away' from your general cleaning.

Refrigerator—Interior

This is not usually a weekly cleaning task. However, if you want to do it on a weekly basis, do it first.

If you are going to clean the freezer part of the refrigerator turn it off sufficiently in advance to allow all the ice to melt (if your freezer is not frost-free). The best time to clean your refrigerator is when it has the least amount of items in it. So you should schedule this task to occur before you do your shopping.

Start with a rubbish bag and throw out everything that you can reasonably part with.

If you are doing the freezer, start by putting any loose ice and ice trays in the sink. If possible do not remove anything else. Instead, move all of the items to the right and spray the left side with Red Liquid and wipe. Now move the items to the left and repeat. If your freezer is heavily stocked, remove only as many items as is necessary.

To clean the refrigerator itself start with the top shelf. The items on the shelves should not be removed, just moved to the right. Use the Red Liquid and the white pad/sponge to clean the shelves. If the shelves are too full, remove only as many items as necessary. These can be placed on a convenient counter or on a clean towel on the floor in front of the refrigerator. Once the shelf is clean, replace the items in the order they were removed.

Continue by doing each subsequent lower shelf until you have finished. Remove the drawers to wipe behind them and clean them thoroughly before replacing.

Clean the door shelves by removing a few items and cleaning under them. Then slide the remaining items over and clean under them. Slide the items back and replace the items removed. Wipe the bottom of each item removed so it does not make a mark on the shelf.

Stove Top Hood

First wipe down the hood, always starting at the top. This will almost always need to be sprayed and wiped—use your Red Liquid or a bicarbonate soda and vinegar combination, which is perfect to remove fatty residues.

Stove Stop

As you are working to the right, clean the left burners using the white pad/sponge as needed. You may also need to use the scraper. Clean the middle of the stove top and then the right burners.

Stove Front

First clean the burner control knobs using the Red Liquid and the toothbrush. If you need to remove the knobs, clean the front of the stove behind them and wipe the surface dry before replacing the knobs.

Now open the door of the oven and clean the inside of the oven door window. To do this first spray with Red Liquid and then use the razor-blade scraper to remove the dirt. You should clean this window even if you are not going to clean the inside of the oven.

Clean the rest of the door and front of the oven only as needed.

Oven—Interior

Put on your gloves and clean the inside of the oven door with a green pad/sponge and Red Liquid. Use a razor-scraper and Blue Liquid to clean the glass in the door. Pull the top rack out to the locked position so that it is easier to clean with your green pad and the powder and liquid of your choice. As you finish cleaning each rack remove it and place it in the sink and rinse it thoroughly. You can place a couple of cloths on the edge of the sink to support the racks and stop them scratching the sink. When you have finished, leave them to dry in the sink.

Now do the inside of the oven starting with the inside top. Use your green pad and a combination of the powder and cleaner you have selected from the recipes. Agitate back and forth with the green pad until the entire baked-on residue on the top of the oven has been loosened. Do not worry about removing any of this yet. Continue to clean, doing the right side, then the back, the left side and finally the bottom. If there are baked-on clumps use your scraper first, do not waste time trying to remove these with a sponge.

As you will have noticed, your green pad became a disgusting mess moments after you started to clean. Resist the temptation to go to the sink and rinse it out. It will just become disgusting the moment you start to clean again and it will work just as well dirty. If the pad becomes difficult to hang on to, fold it in half, and, if needed, squeeze it into the bottom of the oven. Do anything necessary to avoid making trips to the sink to rinse it. When it is impossible to grip the pad, then you can rinse it. Also, if it becomes clogged with debris, you can rinse it. But in general, resist the impulse to go to the sink.

Once you have completely gone over the inside of the oven you can rinse the pad and scraper and put them back into your apron. Now wipe out the inside of the oven with something disposable—old cloths that are no longer viable for cleaning are a good choice or paper towels. Wipe out in the reverse order. Start with the bottom, then left side, back, right side and finally top. You will need to wipe out the entire oven thoroughly once, tossing the soiled cloths to one side as you go. Now spray the entire inside of the oven with Red Liquid, wipe clean and dry with a cloth. Pick up your soiled cloths, close the door and you are finished.

Kitchen Island

If you have a kitchen island this is the time to clean it. Wipe the top first and then the sides if needed.

Remember

Never, ever, return to do something. Do each thing in order, every time.

Kitchen Sink & Dishwasher

As we started at the sink, after working our way around the kitchen, we should now be back at the kitchen sink. If there are dishes in the sink, see that they are done now or placed into the dishwasher.

Clean the splash back of the sink first and then the bowl. You will need to use an appropriate cleaner. For instance, if you have a stainless steel sink you can make up one of the recipes for stainless steel.

Ensure you wipe the front of your dishwater, also clean the machine's seals and handle thoroughly. If the dishwasher is empty run a hot water cycle with 1 cup of vinegar and ½ cup bicarbonate soda to allow it to internally self clean.

Floor

The next step is to vacuum the floor. After this, depending on the type of floor, you can mop or use a floor cleaner/polisher as appropriate.

Empty and replace your rubbish bins and you are done. You should now move on to the bathroom.

The Bathroom

Bathroom

You will need to stock your carry caddy with the following items:

- 1 Container of powder cleaner

- 1 White pad/sponge

- 1 Blue Liquid spray bottle

- 1 Red Liquid spray bottle

- 1 Toilet brush

- 1 Tile brush

- 10 Cleaning cloths

- 2 Microfibre cloths/sponges

- 1 Feather duster

- 1 Whisk broom

- 1 Tile cleaner small squeeze bottle

The following items go in your apron:

- 1 Scraper

- 1 Toothbrush

- 1 Razor-blade scraper

- 2 Plastic bags with clips

WHERE TO START?

Place the carry caddy on the floor at the right side of the bath then work to the right as you clean the bathroom. Put your tools in your apron and tie it firmly around your waist.

Put any rubbish containers outside the bathroom. Then pick up any mats or rugs and put them outside the bathroom, flat on the floor.

Remove any items from the bath and put them on the floor. Put any wet items, such as a bar of soap, on top of a folded cloth on the floor.

Remember, always work from the top to the bottom. Begin with the walls of the shower or bath, using the tile recipe and tile brush. The tile cleaner has all natural ingredients so you do not have to worry about inhaling toxic fumes. As always, only clean the areas that are dirty.

Start with the tile that is furthest from the drain and continue until all the areas that require cleaning are complete.

The soap dish will need to be cleaned with the toothbrush. Start with the handle first and scrape out any soap scum, then use the bristle end to finish off the dish.

Do not rinse yet, do the inside of the doors first.

Shower Doors Inside and Runners

Use your tile liquid on the inside of the shower doors. Take your white pad/sponge and clean the glass. Next take your Red Liquid and toothbrush and clean the runner/tracks. Once these tracks are clean, they will only need wiping.

You are still not ready to rinse yet.

Tub

A microfibre cloth or glove is perfect for cleaning the bath itself, you only need water or white vinegar. You can also use your tile brush to clean the bath with one of your bath cleaning recipes. When you get to the taps/faucets you will need to use your toothbrush to reach the places where the metal meets the tile.

Put your tile brush in the bathroom sink.

Rinse it Out

Now you can rinse the inside of your bath or shower. Start at the top of the wall furthest from the drain and spray all the walls first. Now rinse the doors, finishing at the end of the bath away from the drain, then rinse the bath itself.

Shower Doors Outside

The shower door side, which faces the bathroom, is next. Use the Blue Liquid and cloth to clean this. To get it dry and streak free you can use a dry cloth.

Bathroom Basin—The Bowl

With the tile brush already in the basin, turn on the water and wet the bowl. There should be plenty of tile cleaner still on the brush. You can use this to clean the bowl of the basin. Once the basin is clean; rinse. You have not cleaned the taps, drain, or rim of the basin as yet. That can be done on your second trip round the bathroom.

Toilet—The Bowl

Sprinkle with your chosen toilet bowl cleaner and use a toilet bowl brush to clean by starting high on the inside of the rim. Use a circular motion to clean the bowl. Clean as far down into the bowl as possible. Excess water on the brush should be removed by shaking the brush into the toilet. Now, flush the toilet.

Another Lap

We are now going to move around the room again, this time focusing on surfaces and glass.

Start by placing a dry cloth over your shoulder as we did in the kitchen. Continue to work to the right.

Mirrors

Use the Blue Liquid and a dry cloth to clean mirrors. Spray them lightly, do not over spray. Use the dry cloth to completely dry the mirror, which will eliminate streaks. Remember to replace your Blue Liquid after each use.

Doors

Check for cobwebs at the top of the door frame and remove with the feather duster. There are three primary places to check on a door. The first is at the top of the door frame for cobwebs. The second place to check is the door handle and the frame near it for fingerprints or smudges. The last place to check is near the bottom of the door where someone may have left marks with their shoes when pushing it open.

Cobwebs

Learn to look at the line between your ceiling and wall for cobwebs. Whenever you see these, use your feather duster to remove them. Check any point in a room where two surfaces meet, especially in locations that are out of the normal traffic pattern.

Towel Racks

Remember all towel racks! Use your toothbrush and Red Liquid to clean these quickly, then wipe with a cloth to dry.

Medicine Cabinet

Start at the top as always by wiping the top of the medicine cabinet. Next clean the mirror. Work your way down, cleaning items like the toothbrush holder as you go.

Bathroom Basin—Taps and Drain

Use the Red Liquid to clean the taps and basin drain. Use the toothbrush at the base and edges of the brass/chrome/metal. Use a dry cloth for the final wipe. Do not take the time to dry the entire basin, unless it is stainless steel or glass, just dry the metal fittings.

Toilet – Exterior

The entire exterior of the toilet is next. Start with the top of the cistern (always top to bottom!). Remember to always wipe the flushing handle or button as you pass it.

Start with the toilet seat and lid in the up position. Use the Red Liquid and a cloth or microfibre glove. Spray the underside of the seat, put it down, and then spray the top of the seat. Now spray the underside of the lid, and put it down. The top of the seat is now exposed, so spray this and the hinges and the small flat porcelain surface at the back of the lid.

To complete the process, simply reverse your actions, starting with the small porcelain surface. You will want to use your toothbrush on the small hinges and rubber grommets.

The lid and seat should now be back up.

This leaves the top of the bowl clear so spray this and work your way down the outside of the bowl to the floor. Wipe clean and dry.

Bathroom Floor

While at the base of the toilet, clean the bathroom floor (excluding any carpets). Take several cloths and the Red Liquid, start at the corner nearest the toilet and spray and wipe your way out of the bathroom. When you pass the items you removed from the bath or shower earlier you should put these back.

With this you are finished, at least for a while.

LIVING ROOM

Where To Start?

When you enter the room, place your carry caddy to the right side. You are going to work around this room to your right. You will lead yourself around the room with your feather duster. Start dusting at the top of the wall, looking for cobwebs. As you move around the room clean any dirt you encounter.

Cobwebs

Take your feather duster and go around the room removing all the cobwebs. If you encounter spiders place them outside.

Fingerprints

While removing dust and cobwebs from the door frames check for fingerprints and smudges. When you see these take your Red Liquid and a cloth and clean them.

Pictures with Glass

If you have pictures with glass coverings you should only need to clean these a few times a year. If you want to check to see if they are clean, take a clean dry cloth and wipe them lightly. If you see any streaks they need cleaning. Take your Blue Liquid and a cloth. Spray lightly and wipe clean. Take a dry cloth and dry completely or you will leave streaks. If you have done it correctly you will not have to repeat it for weeks or even months.

Mirrors

Only clean the mirrors if they are dirty. Look for fingerprints and smudges. If they need cleaning, use the Blue Liquid and a cloth. Spray the mirror lightly, as with all glass surfaces, and then wipe dry with a clean cloth.

Marks on the Walls

Remember to check for marks on the walls as you dust. Pay particular attention to the areas of the wall nearest the floor. Clean wall marks with your Red Liquid and a clean cloth.

Surfaces

Whether it is an end table or other surface near a wall, clean above the surface before you clean the surface. If there are no fingerprints, smudges or spills on the surface, simply dust with a damp cloth (or your feather duster). Use your furniture cleaner recipe to clean these surfaces.

If there are objects on the surface, remember to clean from the top down. Clean the object by dusting or wiping, then move it to the other end of the surface and clean the exposed area. Replace the object and clean the other end of the surface.

If the surface is covered with glass, remember to use Blue Liquid, spray lightly and wipe clean. Then use a dry cloth as always and make certain the surface is completely dry.

Fabric Furniture

Start as always from the top and work down. There are many types of fabric and hair will cling to some more than others. You will have to look at your particular furniture fabric and decide how much cleaning is needed.

To start, take the whisk broom and brush from the top down. When you get to the cushions start on the left hand side and brush from the back to the front, working toward the right side. Pick up a couple of the cushions and look under them. If needed, remove each cushion and starting on the left side, take your whisk broom and brush out all the crumbs, pet hair, and other interesting things that accumulate in our furniture.

You also need to decide whether to vacuum the fabric of the couch. If it is due for a vacuum, select an attachment without a beater brush, as this can damage the fabric.

If you do decide you need to vacuum the couch, do not waste your time whisking, and just go straight to vacuuming.

Leave one cushion turned up if you have decided to vacuum the piece of furniture. Then when you do the vacuuming you will remember to do it. This also works to let anyone cleaning with you know that you would like the piece of furniture vacuumed.

Leather Furniture

Start with the whisk broom and brush the chair or sofa from top to bottom. Leather is especially prone to damage from dirt and dust working their way into the creases and seams. For these locations you can use the toothbrush first to loosen the embedded dirt and then the whisk broom to remove the dirt from the chair.

Plants

Use your feather duster or a damp cloth to dust any plants, working from top to bottom. As you finish, pick up dead leaves and put them in your plastic-lined apron pocket. If the plant is too heavy to move, use a cloth and the Red Fluid to clean around its base. Make certain to clean behind the plant if the vacuum cleaner will not reach.

The Home

Curtains or Blinds

Using your feather duster remove dust from blinds and from the top of the curtains and curtain rods. If you live near a busy street or main road be sure to wear a mask to cover your mouth and nose as you clean, otherwise you will be inhaling outside pollutants and heavy metals in the process, which can damage your fertility.

Window Frames

Open the curtains or blinds and dust all window frames.

Bookshelves

Start at the top of the bookshelf and dust the top of the books, if there is room, with your feather duster. Next dust the fronts of the bookshelves. Do not let your duster become too full of dust. Whack it against your shoe near the floor. Then you can easily vacuum up the dust that falls off.

Fireplace

Never use a feather duster on the fireplace mantel or hearth. Soot will ruin your duster and is almost impossible to completely remove. These areas should be left for the small attachment of your vacuum cleaner.

Surfaces in the Middle of the Room

Now you have worked your way round the outside of the room turn your attention to any surfaces in the middle of the room that need cleaning. To clean a table, spray your furniture cleaner/polisher onto the surface evenly, then wipe in the direction of any grain with a clean cloth. This helps to hide any streaks left by your cleaning and polishing. When the surface is almost dry, turn your cloth over and wipe in large sweeping motions, remembering to follow the grain.

FAMILY/LIVING ROOM

The family room is often very well used and can get some heavy traffic so pay special attention to optimising your cleaning in this room.

TV, DVD Player and Stereo

Clean the case of the TV with a duster. This includes the back and sides. Use your Blue Fluid and a clean cloth for the screen. Use a dry cloth to thoroughly dry the screen to avoid leaving streaks. For the DVD player, first dust it with the feather duster and if there are fingerprints use your Red Fluid and cloth to wipe them away. Use the feather duster on the stereo and clean any plastic areas with your already damp furniture polish cloth.

Telephone

Telephones are used so frequently that they almost always need cleaning. You can use the already damp furniture polishing cloth. Do not spray the phone directly—just use your toothbrush to clean small crevices. Clean and polish the base of the phone and lastly the receiver. This will reduce the number of fingerprints you leave.

Piano

Use a duster to remove dust from the top of the piano and work down. Close the cover over the keys before starting to avoid moving dust into the key area. With furniture polish and a furniture polishing cloth, wipe any fingerprints from the surface of the piano. The keys are most likely made from plastic, ivory or ivorite. Plastic keys have no lines, ivorite has evenly spaced lines, and ivory keys have slightly uneven lines. Do not spray the keys. For plastic keys dampen a cloth with a glycerine recipe, for ivorite keys use white vinegar or hydrogen peroxide and for ivory use sweet almond oil. The almond oil will also help prevent the ivory from cracking.

Throw Rugs

Begin by stepping on one end of the throw rug. This will help hold it in place. Vacuum away from where you are standing.

DINING ROOM

Where To Start?

When you enter the living room set your carry caddy on the floor to the right of the door. As always, work to your right and from the top to the bottom.

Items usually unique to dining rooms are a china cabinet/dresser/ sideboard and the dining table and chairs.

Sideboard or Buffet

Using your feather duster or damp cloth dust the top of the sideboard. If it has a glass or mirror vertical surface, use your Blue Liquid and a clean cloth to clean any fingerprints. Spray lightly and wipe thoroughly with a dry cloth to avoid streaks. If there is rubbish on the sideboard, put it in the apron pocket with the plastic liner. Use the appropriate cleaning solution for any flat surfaces and dust around the legs with your feather duster or damp cloth.

Dining-room Table

If your dining room table does not have a tablecloth covering it you should polish it every time you clean. While you polish the first half of the table, dust the chairs that are closest to you. Repeat this on the other end of the dining table. If your chairs have curved legs make sure you remember to dust those as well. Also check the cross supports on the chairs and other flat surfaces and dust them if needed.

ENTRY HALL

Treat the entry hall just like any other room—work to the right, starting with the duster at the point where the wall meets the ceiling, keeping a lookout for cobwebs. There is often a small table in the entry hall, we will either dust this, or clean it in the same way as the tables in other rooms.

HALLWAY

Work down the hall in the same way as usual, top to bottom and to the right. There are often many doors and frames to check for dust and cobwebs. Check the doors for fingerprints and smudges at the usual places.

BEDROOMS

Start with the first bedroom you come to as you go down the hall. As always work to the right and from top to bottom. Start above the door you have just entered, dusting the frame for cobwebs. Remember you will sometimes need to vacuum under the bed, but not every time you clean.

Bedrooms should be straight forward to cleans they should have as little as possible within them. When preparing for a conception it is important to reduce the amount of electromagnetic radiation in the bedroom, this means minimising the amount of electric and electronic devices found there—for more information on this visit www.boostyourfertilitynow.com. However, this is also great news for cleaning—less stuff means less cleaning effort.

Blinds

Your feather duster will be the best tools for this job.

To start, lower the blinds to their full length. Now turn the slats so that the curve is away from you. Grasp the bottom of the blinds at the point where the string that supports the slats intersects. Pull the blinds out from the window and using your feather duster, dust the back of the blinds. Use long slow smooth downward strokes. Dust falls because of gravity and with slow strokes you will be able to catch much of the dust in your duster. Stop the duster at the bottom of your stroke. Tap the duster against your shoe near the floor. The dust will settle to the floor to be vacuumed. Turn the slats forward and repeat the process.

If you live near a busy street or main road be sure to wear a mask to cover your mouth and nose as you clean, otherwise you will be inhaling outside pollutants and heavy metals in the process, which can damage your fertility.

STUDY

Computer

Clean the case of the monitor with a duster. This includes the back and sides. Use Blue Fluid and a clean cloth for the monitor screen. Use a dry cloth to thoroughly dry the screen to avoid leaving streaks. Do not spray anything into the vents of the monitor.

Do not spray the keyboard. Spray Red Liquid onto a cloth and wipe the keys. You can also use compressed air to remove crumbs and dust from between the keys. Do not vacuum the keys as this can dislodge key covers and other small parts and you will have to search through your vacuum for the part.

The computer case can also be cleaned with a cloth that has been sprayed with Red Liquid. Again, do not spray anything into or onto the computer case. The vent on the computer case can be dusted with compressed air. Do not use the vacuum.

Mouse

Wipe the mouse with a cloth that has been sprayed with Red Liquid. If the mouse is a ball type, turn the mouse over and twist the ball cover and remove. Wipe the ball with your cloth and use compressed air to blow debris from the mouse. You may also need to use a toothpick-type instrument to pick out lint that has caught on the rollers inside the mouse. Replace the ball and cover. You may also need to wipe the cord that leads to the mouse. Pick up the mouse pad and tap it on your knee to loosen any dust. Then, if it is plastic, you can use your cloth to clean it.

Photocopier/Printer

The outside of this can be cleaned with a cloth sprayed with Red Liquid. There may also be a glass plate, which can be cleaned by very lightly spraying Blue Liquid onto the glass surface and wiping with a dry cloth. Make certain to dry the glass completely as streaks will show. Do not spray into the vents of this device.

Stairs

With stairs it is especially important to start at the top and vacuum from there down. Put your vacuum cleaner on a convenient step for the length of your hose attachment. Vacuum each step from back to front. If you have a carpeted riser, vacuum this first on each step. When you reach the step on which your vacuum cleaner is sitting, move it down and repeat the process. As you move you can use the whisk broom to clean out crevices and difficult to pick up small items from the corners. Start by whisking several steps and then going back and vacuuming down to the same step.

VACUUMING EFFICIENTLY

The most important rule is to plug the vacuum cleaner in only once and then vacuum the entire house. Studies show that doing just this one thing will reduce the time spent vacuuming by 20% or more.

Use your 20 metre (50 foot extension cord), which is stored on a cord caddy so it does not become tangled. Select a power point as close to your starting point as possible that still allows you to vacuum your entire home.

Your cord should always be behind you. Do not work towards the cord.

Plug the vacuum cleaner cord into the extension cord and unwind most of the extension cord into a neat circular pile that will unravel and not tangle as you vacuum. Plug the extension cord into the power point. Now you have already saved yourself 20% of your vacuuming time, vacuum to the right as with all the work. Be systematic in your vacuuming so you do not miss any areas or, just as importantly, do an area more than once. For example, divide your living room into three equal parts. You can use your furniture as reference points to make certain you do not overlap.

Vacuum with one hand so that your other hand is free to move objects out of your way and always keep yourself directly behind your vacuum cleaner , pushing it forward and then pulling it back. Move to the side almost one full width of the vacuum with each backwards motion.

DOING THE WASHING

Before doing the washing check the inside of the washing machine for loose items such as coins. Have a small basket or tray near your washing machine in which to place these items. Remember to check the lint catcher to make sure it is not full or blocked. This will make your washing machine function better and your clothes come out cleaner.

Ideally you should have five baskets into which to sort your laundry. Colour coding the baskets can be very useful. The baskets are for whites, colourfast items, dark items, linens and towels and one for items that need to be hand washed.

Use a natural stain remover on any stains as quickly as possible. The longer the stain sits, the more difficult it is to remove.

Removing grease

Using the recipe for the grease remover of your choice, rub it into the stain, and then wash.

Laundry Detergent & Natural Stain Remover

There are a number of recipes from which you can select to create the detergent you will use.

An excellent commercial alternative is the Miracle Wash Laundry Ball found at www.boostyourfertilitynow.com. These laundry balls are safe and inexpensive and contain:

- No sodium lauryl sulphate

- No petrochemicals

- No harsh detergents

- No toxic chemicals

- No animal testing

The product has undergone significant testing to ensure that it is not harmful to the environment and is safe for your family's clothes.

Delicates

If you are going to place delicates in your washing machine, place them in a mesh bag. This reduces the chances they will be damaged during the wash cycle.

Soaking

Always check the garment care instructions, as soaking can cause shrinking or other damage. The amount of time you soak a garment depends not only on the garment but also on the cleaner you are adding to the water. In general, most soaking times should be less than one hour, unless specifically called for by the manufacturer.

Inside Out

For most of your clothes it will make little difference if they are turned inside out or not. However, clothes that have printed designs, or a tendency to fade, may fare better in the wash if turned inside out.

Colour Fast

Check and follow the care instructions regarding the colour fastness of all garments before washing. If you are unsure whether a garment is colour fast, check by taking a cloth dampened with vinegar and placing it on an inconspicuous location on the garment. Iron the cloth and if colour transfers on to the cloth, the garment is not colourfast.

CLEANING ALL SURFACES

Laminate, Granite, Stainless Steel and Corian

Use white vinegar or any appropriate recipe. If you have a tough stain, use bicarbonate of soda on your white pad/sponge and scrub vigorously. Don't forget to use the scraper for stuck-on lumps. Remember to dry thoroughly to avoid streaks.

Marble

Never use full strength vinegar on marble. The vinegar can react with the marble and cause pitting and other damage. If you are going to use vinegar as a marble cleaner it should be one part vinegar to five parts water. In all cases you should rinse thoroughly and dry completely.

One Last Note On Shelves

The general rule when cleaning shelves is to remove no more than is absolutely necessary. If at all possible, take whatever is on the shelf and stack it on the right. Clean the left side. Then move the object to the left and clean the right. Finally place the objects back in their original position. You should only remove items from the shelf if absolutely necessary. When removing items, first look for a nearby surface that is clear and about waist high, for instance a counter in the kitchen. Alternatively, place the items on a clean towel on the floor in front of the shelf. When you have finished cleaning the shelf replace the items in the order they were removed.

This may seem a bit counter intuitive initially, but it will save an immense amount of time compared to removing everything from a shelf and then replacing it.

Natural Cleaning
Recipes

Natural Cleaning Recipes

GENERAL PURPOSE CLEANERS

GENERAL-PURPOSE CLEANER (BASE RECIPE)

This formula does double duty for it not only cleans, but the essential oils provide a heavenly fragrance, which will boost your spirits while you clean.

Ingredients:

- 2 **cups hot water**
- 2 **teaspoons borax**
- 1 **teaspoon washing soda**
- ½ **teaspoon liquid soap or detergent**

Up to 1 teaspoon essential oil such as thyme, rosemary, eucalyptus, cinnamon, birch, lavender, tea-tree, sweet orange, rose, lemon grass, or clove.

Yields: 450ml

Time to make: about 10 minutes
Shelf life: Indefinite
Storage: Spray bottle or glass jar with a tightly-fitting lid.

Method:

Combine the water, borax, washing soda and liquid soap in a spray bottle. Secure lid tightly, and mix well by shaking vigorously for about a minute, then add the essential oil you have chosen, and mix well again.

How To Use:

Spray unto the surface you want to clean and let stand about 15 minutes, and then wipe clean with a soft cloth. Waiting the additional 15 minutes before you wipe off the surface allows the qualities of the essential oil time to act.

Variations for the basic recipe:

Some Sweetness:

Mix in ½ teaspoon cinnamon and ½ teaspoon clove essential oils.

A Little Lavender:

Add 1 teaspoon lavender essential oil.

Essentially Orange:

Mix in 1 teaspoon sweet orange essential oil.

Pine Tree Forest:

Mix in 1 teaspoon pine oil.

Note: pine oil is known as a disinfectant and can be used as the essential oil in this recipe, but remember that some people are allergic to pine so it should be used with care.

HARD WATER AID (ACID CLEANER)

In parts of the country where hard water is a problem this cleaner is perfect, as it will help dissolve mineral build-up.

It works especially well for cleaning up after children and pets, or if you have an ill person in the home. It will deodorise and neutralise most bodily fluids.

Ingredients:
- ¾ **cup warm water**
- ¼ **cup white distilled lemon juice or vinegar**
- ½ **teaspoon liquid detergent**

Yields: 225ml

Time to make: About 10 minutes

Shelf life: Indefinite with vinegar, or a few days with lemon juice

Storage: Spray bottle or a glass jar with a spray top. If you choose to make it using lemon juice, which will add a delightful fragrance, remember to store it in the refrigerator.

Method:

Combine the water, lemon juice or vinegar, and liquid detergent in a spray bottle. Make sure the lid is tightly secured, and shake vigorously.

How To Use:

Generously spray affected area and wipe clean with a soft cloth.

DON'T FORGET THE SOAP AND WATER

It is easy to forget one of the best cleaners of all time—natural, vegetable oil derived soap.

Ingredients:

   2 **cups warm water**
28 gm **liquid (or bar) castile soap**

Makes: One 450ml bottle

Time to make: About 5 minutes using liquid soap, or about 12 hours using bar soap.

Shelf life: Indefinite

Storage: Spray bottle

A note on mixing:

Creating this formula with liquid soap is by far the least time consuming, as you won't have to wait as long for it to dissolve. However, when you use bar soap you will be re-living history by mixing your soap the way our ancestors did.

Mixing using Liquid Castile Soap:

Combine water and soap in a spray bottle, mix well.

Mixing using bar soap:

In a glass jar combine water and soap, allow to stand overnight or until the soap is dissolved. Shake occasionally. Once it is dissolved pour it into a spray bottle.

How To Use:

Remember to shake between each use. Mist onto stain or surface to be cleaned and wipe with a clean soft cloth.

MILDEW BE-GONE

An excellent mildew buster is found in the simple ingredient, tea-tree oil.

Ingredients:

- 1 **cup water**
- 1 **teaspoon tea-tree oil**
- ¼ **teaspoon liquid soap or detergent**

Yields: 225ml

Time to make: about 5 minutes
Shelf life: Indefinite
Storage: Spray bottle or glass jar with a tightly-fitting lid

Method:

Combine the water, tea-tree oil, and liquid soap in a spray bottle, secure the lid tightly and mix well by shaking the bottle.

How To Use:

Spray onto affected surface but do not immediately rinse off. Allow to set for about three days while the tea-tree oil does its job. The strong scent of the tea-tree oil will dissipate in a few days.

SODA CLEANER

So simple and easy, you will use it again and again.

One ingredient only:

1 cup soda water

Yields: 225ml

Time to make: about 1 minute
Shelf life: Indefinite
Storage: Spray or soda bottle

Method:

Just pour one cup of soda water into your favourite spray bottle!

The great thing about soda water is that it really works because it contains alkaline minerals.

How To Use:

Spray on surface and wipe clean with a soft cloth.

ALL-PURPOSE DEGREASER

Perhaps you have a loved one who loves cars and engines?

This fantastic cleaner is just what you need to tackle super-tough grease stains. It will even remove motor oil.

Ingredients:

- 2 **cups hot water**
- 4 **teaspoons washing soda**
- 4 **teaspoons borax**
- 1 **teaspoon liquid soap or detergent**

Yields: 450ml

Time to make: About 10 minutes
Shelf life: Indefinite
Storage: Spray bottle

Method:

Combine water, washing soda, borax, and liquid soap in a spray bottle. Secure lid and shake well.

How To Use:

Spray on stain and wipe dry.

Note: the large amount of washing soda may leave a white residue, so be sure to rinse well with clean water.

THE BIG JOB CLEANER

If you feel inspired to take on a huge job, or a relative is visiting and you want everything to be spotless – try this outstanding cleaner.

Ingredients:

> 9 **litres hot water**
> ¼ **cup borax**
> ¼ **cup liquid soap**
> ¼ **cup washing soda**

Yields: 9.5L

Time to make: About 10 minutes
Shelf life: Discard after use
Storage: Discard after use

Tip:

For ease of measuring, use a clean, empty, one-litre bottle to measure the water and you can use a broom handle or a stick for mixing.

Method:

Combine water, borax, liquid soap, and washing soda in a large bucket (available from hardware stores) and mix well until dissolved. Use a broom handle or stick from the garden to mix.

How To Use:

Being sure to wear gloves, dip a clean rag into the solution, wring out excess moisture and wash the surface you want to clean. Don't forget to remoisten your rag frequently. Tip: Keep an extra rag and bucket filled with clean water on hand. You can use the water to rinse the surface once you are done.

SOAP WITH VINEGAR CLEANER

A superb cleaner for areas that are difficult to rinse. It is also an exceptionally good cleaner for the bathroom, as the vinegar will help fight mildew and mineral build-up.

Ingredients:

> 9 **litres water**
> ½ **cup white vinegar**
> ¼ **cup liquid soap**

Yields: 9.5L

Time to make: About 10 minutes
Shelf life: Indefinite
Storage: Spray bottle

Tip:

For ease of measuring, use a clean, empty, one-litre bottle to measure the water and you can use a broom handle or a stick for mixing.

Method:

Combine water, borax, liquid soap, and washing soda in a large bucket (available from hardware stores) and mix well until dissolved.

How To Use:

Being sure to wear gloves, dip a clean cloth into the solution, wring out excess moisture and wash the surface you want to clean. Don't forget to re-moisten your cloth frequently. There is no need to rinse!

WALL CLEANERS

No matter what kind of wallpaper or paint you have in your home, it is always recommended that you first test any cleaner in a small unobtrusive spot. If in doubt, consult the manufacturer, or the store where the wall covering was purchased, for safe cleaning instructions.

HINTS AND TIPS FOR CLEANING WALLS

Washing walls is the only place you can break the 'always work from top to bottom' rule. You have probably experienced washing your walls only to find that as you reached the bottom there are drip lines always just ahead of you, and by the time you reach them they have dried and become difficult to remove.

This problem can be eliminated when you use the 'bottom, up' approach. Rub non-washable-wallpaper and paints with a pencil eraser or artist gum eraser to remove stains or spots. For a more natural alternative try rubbing the stalk of freshly-cut rhubarb over the stain and wiping with a lightly moistened cloth. Remember to test on a hidden area first before using either method on a visible area.

To remove grease stains, tear or cut a paper towel into four pieces, apply one or two drops of eucalyptus essential oil to each piece and let them dry. Turn your iron on to a low setting and press an oil-treated towel square against the stain. Repeat with the remaining paper towel pieces.

If the grease stain still remains, wait a few hours and then apply a thick paste made from cream of tartar, baking soda, and water. Mix by adding water until the cream of tartar and baking soda stick together. Once the paste has dried to a powder, brush it away with a soft cloth. If neither of these techniques has worked you might want to consider painting over or, in the case of wallpaper, patching the spot.

Luckily the crayons manufactured today are safe, non-toxic and in most cases washable. But if some crayon scribbles from a non-washable crayon have found their way onto your wall, try the techniques described for removing grease stains. If they fail and the crayon is on a painted surface, try scrubbing the surface with a liquid castile soap to which you have added 1 or 2 drops of orange essential oil. This is not a technique recommended for wallpaper.

One of our most disheartening tasks when cleaning walls can come from food stains, which some way or other always seem to find their way onto the most difficult-to-clean places. Spaghetti sauce is one of the main culprits as it tends to bubble and leap from the pot. If it is wiped up right away it is usually not a problem, however we often don't notice the stains until we are cleaning. If the walls are covered in washable paint, it should be relatively easy to wipe them off with All-purpose Cleaner. However, if the walls are painted with latex paint the stains may be harder to remove. First, if necessary, scrape with your spatula or a blunt knife, and then use an organic cotton ball with a few drops of eucalyptus oil on it. Dip the cotton ball into sodium bicarbonate and rub the stain with the cotton ball until the stain disappears.

GENERAL USE WALL CLEANER

Reach for this amazing dirt buster whenever you need to tackle dirt, scuffs, and spots or crayon wall art. It is also perfect for skirting boards, fixtures and countertops.

When mixing your all-purpose cleaner don't overlook natural, mild-on-hands, kitchen dishwashing liquid as an ingredient (do your research to ensure it is a natural product you are purchasing, not just a marketing scheme). The containers make convenient squirt bottles, which can be difficult to find in shops, and recycling those saves money. However, it's easy to use more dishwashing liquid then you really need. So remember, a little goes a long way.

NOTE ON WASHING SODA

Washing soda is sodium carbonate. It is in the same family as bicarbonate soda but it is not the same thing. It is processed differently and is much more caustic/alkaline, with a pH of 11. It does not give off harmful fumes but you should wear gloves when using it. You can usually find it in the laundry section of large supermarkets, often under the brand name 'Lectric Soda'.

Ingredients:
- ½ teaspoon washing soda
- 2 teaspoons borax
- ½ teaspoon liquid soap or detergent
- 2 cups hot water
- Optional: 1 teaspoon orange oil

Yields: 450ml

Time to make: About 10 minutes
Shelf life: Indefinite

Storage: Spray bottle

Method:

Combine the soap, borax, and washing soda in a spray bottle. Add the hot water carefully, secure the lid tightly and shake until well mixed and dissolved.

How To Use:

Spray every twelve centimetres (five inches), or as frequently as needed, wiping off with a cloth as you go.

For stubborn dirt let the cleaner sit on the surface for a few minutes, and then wipe off as before. Remember to shake the bottle each time before using.

The best thing about making your own cleaners at home is that you can spice them up, or add scents to fit the seasons and holidays.

Here are some variations to the basic recipe:

Borax Spray Solution:

When mixing, leave out the washing soda.

Bicarbonate Soda Spray:

For a gentler and less caustic spray, substitute bicarbonate of soda for washing soda.

Salty Cleaner Spray:

For a cleaner that is alkaline, but has non-caustic minerals, substitute Epsom salts for washing soda when mixing.

Soda Water Spray:

When mixing, use only enough hot water to dissolve the minerals, and then add soda water, which contains alkaline minerals.

THREE INGREDIENT WALL CLEANER

This is a very easy and effective cleaner which uses only three basic ingredients. It easily cleans wall surfaces for fresh sparkling results.

Ingredients:

- 1 **cup water**
- ½ **cup vinegar**
- 6 **drops orange, lemon, or grapefruit essential oil**

Yields: 350ml

Time to make: about 5 minutes
Shelf life: 6 months or more
Storage: Spray bottle

Method:

Combine the water, vinegar and essential oil in a spray bottle and shake vigorously.

How To Use:

Remember to shake well before each use. Spray the stain lightly and wipe with a soft cloth. If the stain is still visible after it has completely dried, see tips for cleaning walls.

CLEANING THYME

This thyme-based formula makes a wonderful disinfectant for general purposes and that is also perfect for safely cleaning wall surfaces in a child's room. It also works well on cribs, light switches, or wherever those darling little fingers have left germs or smudges.

Ingredients:

> 1 **cup water**
> 1 **cup vinegar**
> 5 **drops tea-tree essential oil**
> 3 **drops thyme essential oil**

Yields: 450ml

Time to make: About 5 minutes
Shelf life: 6 months or more
Storage: Spray bottle

Method:

Combine the water, vinegar, and essential oils in a spray bottle, secure the lid tightly, and shake well.

How To Use:

Spray lightly and then wipe with a clean, damp, rag. You can give a final wipe with a cloth moistened with plain water.

FRESHLY MINTED WALL CLEANER

This is perfect for dissolving grease and fingerprints that often occur on walls, especially those in the kitchen, bathroom, or children's room. It works best on semi-gloss paint or washable wallpaper. It is non-abrasive, and the small amount of tea-tree oil will not harm coloured wallpapers.

Ingredients:

¼ **cup concentrated oil soap paste (found in natural food or hardware stores)**
2 **drops peppermint essential oil**
2 **drops spearmint essential oil**
2 **drops tea-tree essential oil**

Yields: 50g

Time to make: About 5 minutes
Shelf life: Indefinite
Storage: Small jar

Method:

Begin by putting the soap paste in a small jar (a clean baby food jar works well). Add essential oils one at a time, mixing well after each addition. It should have the consistency of jelly.

How To Use:

Using a clean damp rag, dip into the minty mix and rub the cloth between your fingers until it lathers, then rub on wallpaper or walls. Follow up by rinsing with another damp cloth moistened with plain water. A dry cloth may be used to finish, leaving a beautifully clean surface.

CARPET CLEANERS

Hints and Tips for Carpet Care

Always clean spills up as soon as possible. Make sure you blot the spill with clean white paper towels or clean cotton rags. Never scrub your carpets to remove a stain, as it will cause it to sink further into the fibres of the carpet. Quickly scoop up as much of the spill as you can with a spoon.

For Food Stains:

The majority of stains caused by food can be easily removed with a mixture of vinegar and a bit of natural dishwashing liquid. If you like, you can add a few drops of your favourite essential oil to the vinegar.

For Bloodstains:

Most of the time bloodstains can be removed by blotting them with soda water or cold water. If any of the stain still remains try dampening a cloth with cold water and adding 2 drops of eucalyptus essential oil, then blot the stain again.

For Ink Stains:

Sprinkle the entire carpet thickly with cream of tartar. Slice a wedge of lemon and squeeze the juice onto the cream of tartar. Using the remaining rind, gently rub the spot a few times. Moisten a cloth, brush away the cream of tartar, and dab.

For Urine Stains:

Soak up as much liquid as possible with paper towels. Mix a solution of ¼ cup vinegar, 1 teaspoon dishwashing soap, and 10 drops of eucalyptus essential oil and apply to the affected area with a clean cloth. Let stand for about 25 minutes. The essential oil and vinegar will help sanitise and absorb the odour. Dab the stain again with a clean cloth. Use caution on dark carpets as vinegar can sometimes bleach dark colours.

For Candle Wax:

Using a hairdryer, heat the wax. Be careful not to scorch the carpet. As the wax softens and melts, dab clean with a cloth or rag.

Carpet Don'ts

Never use salt on carpet spills, as it can leave an unsightly white residue.

Do not spray or pour water onto products such as bicarbonate of soda or borax. The residue left by adding water will become a difficult problem to remove. If this does happen it is best to let the minerals dry thoroughly and then vacuum.

If any residue remains, you can spray it with a solution of ½ cup white distilled vinegar and ½ cup water mixed well in a spray bottle. Again, let it dry and then vacuum.

COMMERCIAL RUG CLEANER

If you have ever waited in line at the supermarket you have probably seen those commercial rug cleaning machines for rent, with expensive rug shampoos sitting next to them. The cost of those toxic chemical cleaners can be as much as, or even more than, the price of renting the machine. Here is a simple alternative that is safe for use in commercial steam extraction rug cleaners.

Ingredients:
- **18 litres of water**
- **¼ cup concentrated all-purpose liquid detergent. Be sure it is fragrance-free.**

Yields: 18L

Time to make: About 10 minutes
Shelf life: Discard after use
Storage: Discard after use

How To Use:

Fill the machine's water and detergent dispenser and then follow the manufacturer's instructions.

Variations On The Basic Recipe:

Tough Stain Formula:

The addition of alkaline minerals should help rid the carpet of stubborn dirt and grime. Mix together two teaspoons of borax and two teaspoons of washing soda in about four cups of hot water and pour into the water dispenser of the machine. Be careful when adding minerals as they may leave a white residue and require extra rising.

FUNGUS CARPET SPRAY

Carpets can sometimes become musty smelling. This easy-to-make cleaner is the answer.

Ingredients:

>2 **cups water**
>2 **teaspoons tea-tree oil**

Yields: 450ml

Time to make: About 5 minutes
Shelf life: Indefinite
Storage: Spray bottle

Method:

Combine the water and tea-tree oil in a spray bottle. Secure the lid tightly and blend well.

How To Use:

First test the formula on an out-of-the-way patch of carpet, to make sure it will not stain, and then spray the area liberally. No need to rinse. The strong odour of the tea-tree oil will disappear in a few days.

CARPET DEODORISER

The simplest solutions are so often the best, and this deodoriser is certainly no exception, it works like magic.

Ingredients:

    1kg Bicarbonate soda

Time to make: Nil
Shelf life: Indefinite
Storage: Original container

Method:

      Bicarbonate of soda comes in boxes that the powder can be shaken from. Alternatively you can put inside a flour shaker container.

How To Use:

Sprinkle over the carpet, let stand overnight, and then vacuum. Some odours might require a couple of bicarbonate of soda treatments. A couple of helpful hints to remember when using bicarbonate of soda on carpet:

1.   To avoid a clogged vacuum, sweep as much of the bicarbonate of soda as you can into a dustpan and dispose. Then vacuum as usual.

2.   If any of the bicarbonate of soda becomes damp and leaves a residue on the carpet you can wash it away with a mixture of one cup water and ¼ cup white distilled vinegar.

3.

Variations for Bicarbonate of Soda:

Goodbye Musty Odours:

Substitute borax for bicarbonate of soda if the carpet smells musty.

Herbal Delight:

To add a delightful aroma to your deodoriser, add about 1 tablespoon dry ground herbs or rose petals to every two cups of bicarbonate of soda.

Adios Pet Odours:

Use either borax or bicarbonate of soda, or spray soda water on the spot. Do not rinse, soak up extra dampness with a clean dry rag.

Spilled Milk Deodoriser:

To remove odours caused by beverages such as milk, wine or alcohol, use either borax or bicarbonate of soda or spray pure soda water on the spot. Do not rinse; soak up extra dampness with a clean dry rag.

FOAMING CARPET CLEANER

Indulge yourself in the light and fluffy texture of this delightful carpet cleaner. You will feel as though you are cleaning your carpet with whipped cream!

Ingredients:

- ½ **cup water**
- ½ **cup natural detergent, available from reputable health foods stores**

Yields: Makes enough to cover a 3m x 3m room

Time to make: About 5 minutes
Shelf life: Indefinite, but remember to re-whip before you re-use it.
Storage: Glass jar, or storage container such as Tupperware.

Method:

Whip water and detergent together with a hand mixer until it has a light and frothy texture.

How To Use:

Dip a clean cloth into the mixture, massage it into the carpet, and wipe dry with a clean cloth. Repeat for entire carpet.

EASY SPILL ABSORBER

Ingredients:

> **Cornstarch**

How To Use:

Shake cornstarch over spill and let stand for about 15 minutes. Sweep as much cornstarch as possible into a dustpan (a hand broom is often helpful). Follow up by vacuuming.

WATER WITH VINEGAR

This formula will amaze you with its simplicity and practical uses. The vinegar works as an antiseptic and will neutralise odours such as those left by pets. It will also draw dirt up from deep within the fibres of your carpet so they can be easily sopped up. In addition it is an excellent rinse to follow a detergent.

Ingredients:

> 1 **cup water**
> 1 **cup vinegar**

Yields: 450ml

Time to make: About 5 minutes
Shelf life: Indefinite
Storage: Spray bottle

Method:

Combine water and vinegar in a spray bottle. Secure the lid tightly and shake until blended.

How To Use:

Spray on affected area of carpet. Let stand for about 10 minutes, and then blot solution with clean white paper towels or cotton rags.

Alternatively, dip a clean sponge mop into the water and vinegar solution and squeeze out any extra liquid. Using a back and forth motion very gently rub the carpet with the mop. Wait at least one hour before vacuuming.

The smell of vinegar will disappear in just a few hours.

Tip:

Think of the room in sections and start at the corner of the section furthest from the entrance to the room you are cleaning. This technique will save time and prevent you from being worked into a corner.

SWEET LAVENDER CARPET CLEANER

Its lovely scent will whisk you away to a summer's field bursting into life, as you breathe in the sweet, fresh scent of the lavender and rosemary used in this recipe. You will feel as if you have a garden in your home, no matter what time of year.

Ingredients:

- 2 **cups bicarbonate of soda**
- ½ **cup soap flakes**
- 20 **drops lavender essential oil**
- 8 **drops rosemary essential oil**
- ½ **cup vinegar**
- 2 **cups warm water**

Yields: Makes enough to cover a 3m x 4m room

Time to make: About 10 minutes

Shelf life: Discard after use

Storage: Discard after use

Note: Instead of soap flakes you can substitute half a cup of borax. However, be sure to test in an inconspicuous spot first.

Method:

In a plastic bowl combine soap flakes and bicarbonate of soda and whisk until well blended. To this add the lavender and rosemary essential oils and stir again until well blended, making sure to break up any clumps with the whisk.

Note: Do not use your cooking whisk for mixing these recipes!

How To Use:

Before you begin, go over your carpet with a broom to loosen the dirt, and then vacuum the carpet thoroughly. Sprinkle mixture over carpet; leave for as long as possible—at least 30 minutes and as long as overnight. Sweep as much carpet cleaner as possible into a dustpan (a hand broom is often helpful). Follow up by vacuuming.

LIQUID PEPPERMINT CARPET CLEANER

When the holidays come around, you will adore this formula, not only for its fresh peppermint scent, but also because it works wonders on the high traffic areas of the holiday festivities!

Ingredients:
- ¾ **cup vegetable-based liquid soap**
- 3 **cups water**
- 10 **drops peppermint essential oil**

Yields: 4 cups

Time to make: About 5 minutes
Shelf life: Indefinite
Storage: Glass jar

Method:

Place water, liquid soap, and peppermint essential oil into a bowl and blend until foamy with a hand mixer.

How To Use:

Scoop a generous amount onto a clean cloth and gently rub the solution onto the affected areas. Allow to dry completely and then vacuum.

'FOREST FRESHNESS' CARPET ODOUR REMOVER

This recipe will leave rugs smelling as fresh and clean as a sunny afternoon among the tree tops.

Ingredients:

- 1 **cup borax**
- 1 **cup baking soda**
- ½ **cup cornmeal**
- 10 **drops juniper essential oil**
- 5 **drops cypress essential oil**

Time to make: About 5 minutes
Shelf life: Indefinite
Storage: Glass jar

Method:

In a bowl combine borax, cornmeal, and bicarbonate of soda and whisk until well blended. Add the juniper and cypress essential oils and stir again until well blended, making sure to break up any clumps with the whisk.

Note: Do not use your cooking whisk for mixing these recipes!

How To Use:

Shake over carpet; allow it to stand for a few hours (or for tough odours, overnight), and then vacuum.

HERBAL CARPET REMEDY

Ingredients:

- 2.5 litres hot water
- ½ cup borax
- ¼ cup vinegar
- 8 drops rosemary essential oil
- 3 drops lemon essential oil

Time to make: About 5 minutes
Shelf life: Indefinite
Storage: Glass jar

Method:

Mix water, alum, vinegar, and rosemary and lemon essential oils in a large bucket. Prepare a second bucket by filling it with hot water. This will be used for rinsing.

How To Use:

Begin at the corner of the room furthest from the entrance. This technique will save time and prevent you from being worked into a corner.

Dip a clean sponge mop into the water and vinegar solution and squeeze out any extra liquid. Using a back and forth motion very gently rub the carpet with the mop. Rinse the mop in the second bucket when needed. Continue until you have cleaned the entire area.

Tip:

To spot clean, first rub a small amount of baking soda onto stain, wait about five minutes and then brush with a soft-bristle brush (an old toothbrush works well). Follow up with Herbal Carpet Remedy. Be sure to wear gloves if your hands are going to come into contact with the solution.

NO-FLEA CARPET SOLUTION

You will be flea-free once you have tried this carpet cure. Remember: throw away the vacuum cleaner bag once you have finished vacuuming, to help prevent future infestations.

Ingredients:

- 3 **cups bicarbonate of soda**
- 10 **drops sweet orange essential oil**
- 10 **drops citronella essential oil**
- 8 **drops peppermint or spearmint essential oil**
- 6 **drops lemon balm essential oil**

Time to make: About 5 minutes
Shelf life: Indefinite
Storage: Glass jar

Method:

Combine bicarbonate of soda, sweet orange, citronella, peppermint, and lemon balm essential oils in a large bowl and whisk together.

Note: Do not use your cooking whisk for mixing these recipes!

How To Use:

Shake over carpet and let stand for at least 1 hour, or leave it overnight. Vacuum.

Get Your FREE Bonuses Today!

FREE Fertility Advice from 'The Bringer of Babies'

Leading natural fertility specialist, Gabriela Rosa (aka The Bringer of Babies) has a gift for you. As a thank you for purchasing this book get your FREE "Natural Fertility Booster" subscription and discover...

- Easy ways to comprehensively boost your fertility and conceive naturally, even for women over 40;
- Natural methods to dramatically increase your chances of creating a baby through assisted reproductive technologies such as IUI, IVF, GIFT or ICSI;
- Simple strategies to help you take home a healthier baby;
- How to prevent miscarriages.

You will also receive the FREE audio CD "11 Proven Steps To Create The Pregnancy You Desire And Take Home The Healthy Baby of Your Dreams" a total value of $397!

Claim your bonuses at
www.NaturalFertilityBoost.com

Be quick, this is a limited offer.
(Your free subscription code is: ATCP)

Metal Cleaners

We all enjoy the gleam of perfectly polished silver. Somehow it brings us back to the elegance of the past.

Unfortunately, the silver polishes often used are hazardous and harmful to health and fertility. You might be thinking that a homemade polish could never do the same job as a commercial one, but you will be pleasantly surprised!

Also as a last note of caution. Always wear a mask and gloves when cleaning metals. Although you may have less needs to polish these since it is important that during the 120 days of a preconception program, during conception attempts and throughout pregnancy you avoid continuous use of metal utensils, which come in contact with your foods and drinks—as they often leach into the food and end up in the body and this can play havoc with various aspects of health including fertility. Hopefully there will be no need for you to clean metals if you are not using them in your day to day.

GENERAL PURPOSE METAL RESTORERS

Ashes - Collect ashes from burnt wood; shake on to a moist cloth and polish. Dip in hot water and dry thoroughly with a soft cloth.

Bicarbonate of Soda - In a small bowl combine ½ cup bicarbonate of soda with enough water to make a paste. Dip a clean cloth into the mixture and polish the metal until it shines. Rinse in hot water and dry thoroughly with a soft cloth. Note: Never use bicarbonate of soda to clean aluminium.

Diatomaceous Earth - In a small bowl combine ½ cup diatomaceous earth with enough water to make a paste. Dip a clean cloth into the mixture and polish the metal. Rinse in hot water and dry thoroughly with a soft cloth.

Toothpaste - Squeeze a small amount (about the size of a pea) into your hand, and rub it on until the tarnish disappears.

Vinegar - Mix at least ¼ cup white distilled vinegar with 2 cups water. Place metal piece in a container, pour the mixture over it and allow to soak. If the piece is very tarnished soak in pure vinegar. Lemon juice also works well instead of vinegar. Rinse in hot water and dry thoroughly with a soft cloth.

Natural acids - Found in lime, lemon, and tomato juices and also in vinegar, work well for cleaning metals and are an excellent alternative to harmful acidic polishes.

Aluminium

You should never use bicarbonate of soda or washing soda to clean aluminium. In fact, hopefully, you are not in contact with aluminium at all, because it can affect your health and fertility. It is essential to replace your kettle, pots, pans and utensils with glass or enamelled cast iron, to safeguard your fertility and the health of your family (for more information see The Natural Fertility Solution Take-Home Program available from www.boostyourfertilitynow.com).

VINEGAR METAL CLEANER

Ingredients:

- 1 **cup vinegar**
- 2 **cups boiled water**
- 1 **teaspoon lemon, orange, or lime essential oil**

Time to make: About 5 minutes
Shelf life: Indefinite
Storage: Glass jar

Method:

Combine vinegar, boiled water, and essential oil in a bowl.

How To Use:

Put the metal pieces you want to clean in the bowl and allow to soak for at least an hour.

METAL SCRUB

Ingredients:

- 2 tablespoons cream of tartar
- ¼ cup white distilled vinegar
- 4 drops orange, lime, or lemon essential oil

Time to make: About 5 minutes
Shelf life: Indefinite
Storage: Glass jar

Method:

Combine cream of tartar, vinegar, and essential oil and stir to make a paste.

How To Use:

Wearing protective gloves pour the mixture onto the metal and rub with your fingers until it is clean. Rinse in cool water and dry thoroughly.

RHUBARB TARNISH REMOVER

Ingredients:

> 2 **cups water**
> 1 **cup fresh rhubarb or tomatoes–sliced**

Time to make: About 5 minutes
Shelf life: Use within 5 days
Storage: Glass jar

Method:

Combine water and rhubarb in pot and bring to a boil.

How To Use:

Put the items to be cleaned into the boiling pot and simmer for 30 minutes. Rinse well under cool water and dry thoroughly.

Gabriela Rosa

COPPER, BRASS, AND BRONZE

Understanding Brass

Brass is an alloy of copper and zinc. Nowadays, it is often finished with a coat of lacquer to prevent tarnishing. It is easy to maintain the brilliance of brass with regular dustings and the occasional warm soapy bath. Never wash lacquered brass objects in hot water because it will cause the finish to peel. You can polish brass to a high shine with a cloth moistened with olive oil. As brass begins to age it will oxidise and can become tarnished and acquire a green tint. These recipes in this section will put you on your way to brightly-polished brass.

UNIQUE ITEMS

Antique brass objects need special attention. It is important not to remove the patina, which gives the object an aged look and often increases its value. If you need to clean an antique piece I would recommend a dip in a warm soapy water bath to remove grime and dust then a rub with a soft cloth moistened with linseed oil. Before you try any of the methods described on an antique, fragile, or delicate object it is advisable to consult an expert such as a restoration specialist, museum curator, or antique dealer.

Clean brass and irons with extra-fine steel wool or an emery cloth, remembering to rub in one direction only.

Tips:

1. Natural acids are best to use when cleaning copper, brass, or bronze.

2. To remove the lacquer coating on new copper, brass, and bronze, add 3 teaspoons bicarbonate of soda and 2 teaspoons washing soda to 2 cups of water and bring to the boil.

Immerse the piece in the boiling solution. Wait until the lacquer finish has peeled away and then buff to a bright shine.

ESSENTIAL OIL BRASS POLISH

Cleaning your brass will be a breeze when you use this polish.

Ingredients:

- 4 **drops lemon, orange or lime essential oil**
- 2 **teaspoons salt**
- 1 **cup vinegar**
  Pinch of all-purpose flour

Yields: 1 cup

Time to make: About 5 minutes
Storage: Dispose after use

Method:

Combine essential oil, salt, and vinegar in a bowl. Add a little flour at a time until you have a thick paste.

How To Use:

Rub the paste on the brass with a clean dry sponge. Allow the paste to dry thoroughly, rinse well under warm water. Dry with a clean soft cloth and then buff.

ALMOST GOOD ENOUGH TO EAT BRASS POLISHER

This recipe will leave your brass with a brilliant shine.

Ingredients:

- ¼ **cup Worcestershire sauce**
- ¼ **cup vinegar**
- 3 **drops lemon essential oil**
- 3 **drops grapefruit seed extract.**

Yields: ½ cup

Time to make: About 5 minutes
Storage: Discard after use

Method:

Combine Worcestershire sauce, vinegar, lemon essential oil, and grapefruit seed extract, mix well.

How To Use:

Scoop a small quantity on to a clean dry cloth. Rub the object with the solution. For very tarnished pieces you will need to let the mixture sit for at least 30 minutes. Rinse well and dry with a soft cloth.

SHINING BRASS MILK BATH

Now we know how Cleopatra kept her brass bath tub gleaming!

Ingredients:

> 1   **cup milk**
> 1   **cup water**

Yields: 2 cups

Time to make: About 5 minutes
Storage: Dispose

Method:
Combine milk and water together and stir well. Note: To clean larger pieces simply mix equal parts milk and water in the quantities desired.

How To Use:

In a pan place the pieces you are cleaning. Pour the milk mixture over to cover. Allow to soak until tarnish is removed.

BRASS TAR-TAR

Ingredients:

- ¼ cup lemon juice
- 5 drops lemon or orange essential oil
- 2-3 tablespoons cream of tartar

Yields: 1 cup

Time to make: About 5 minutes

Storage: Discard after use

Method:

Combine lemon juice, essential oil, and cream of tartar in a bowl, mix well.

How To Use:

Using your fingers (be sure to wear protective gloves) massage the paste onto the piece using a smooth circular motion. Allow to dry. Rinse well under cool water and dry thoroughly with a soft cloth.

MULTI-METAL POLISHER

Try this easy-to-make recipe that works really well not only on brass, but also on copper and bronze.

Ingredients:

>   1 **tablespoon flour**
>   3 **teaspoons salt**
>   **White distilled vinegar**

Yields: 4 tablespoons

Time to make: About 5 minutes
Storage: Single use only

Method:

In a small bowl add flour and salt, then, one tablespoon at a time, add the vinegar and stir until you have a smooth paste.

How To Use:

Dip a clean cloth into the paste and rub the metal surface. Rinse in hot water and dry with a clean cloth then polish.

Variations:

To add a different twist, substitute any of the following for vinegar in the basic recipe:

- Lemon juice

- Lime juice

- Tomato juice

- Milk

ANY SAUCE POLISH

One word, YUM! This extremely easy idea works well if you are in a rush.

Choose one:

- Tomato sauce

- Worcestershire sauce

- Lemon wedge

- Lime wedge

Time to make: About 5 minutes
Storage: Single use only

How To Use:

Squeeze a small amount onto a cloth and rub into metal. Rinse in hot water and dry with a clean rag.

Gabriela Rosa

BRONZE

Understanding Bronze

Bronze is any of a broad range of <u>copper</u> alloys, usually with tin as the main additive, but sometimes combined with other elements. It was especially important in antiquity, giving its name to the Bronze Age. Nowadays, solid bronze objects are often given a protective coating of lacquer. High-quality bronze objects and those we leave out of doors will acquire a beautiful weathered patina (greenish colour) as they age. Inexpensive and reproduction pieces often try to mimic this effect, although none really capture its loveliness. Because of this highly-prized patina, bronze requires little attention or cleaning and a regular dusting and light polishing are usually all that is needed. You could also use a soft brush to clean a piece if it has not been well cared for. Bronze may also be afflicted with what is called 'Bronze Disease'. It looks as though the bronze is growing a fuzzy fungus but this is not the case. It is actually corrosion caused by a reaction of cuprous chloride and moisture. Be sure to consult an expert if you become concerned.

150

GREASE BUSTER

Use this mixture to remove grease and grime from bronze.

Ingredients:

>   1   **cup vinegar**
> 1/8   **cup grapefruit juice**
>   6   **drops cedar or pine essential oil**

Time to make: About 5 minutes
Storage: Single use only

Method:

Combine vinegar, grapefruit juice, and essential oil in a bowl and mix well.

How To Use:

Use your fingers (be sure to wear protective gloves) to massage the mixture onto the piece using a smooth circular motion. Allow to dry. Rinse well under cool water and dry thoroughly with a soft cloth.

'BRONZE DISEASE' TREATMENT

Use distilled water to treat mild cases of bronze disease. If it does not work consider consulting an expert.

Method:

Boil the affected piece in the distilled water, changing the water periodically. You may also need to let the piece sit for a few days in distilled water.

Note: Never use tap water as the minerals can make the bronze disease worse.

Tip:

You might also try hot vinegar and salt, or hot buttermilk.

GENERAL-PURPOSE BRASS AND BRONZE CLEANER

TARNISH REMOVING BATH

No time to polish and scrub? Let this brass and bronze bath do the work for you!

Ingredients:

> **White distilled vinegar or another acid. You can substitute:**
> **Lemon juice**
> **Lime juice**
> **Tomato juice**

Time to make: About 5 minutes
Storage: Single use only

Method:

May be mixed with distilled water for larger pieces, but don't exceed a ½ water, ½ acid mixture.

How To Use:

Place metal object to be cleaned in a bucket or your preferred container and pour the tarnish removing solution over it so that it is completely immersed. Allow to stand for four to five hours or overnight.

COPPER

New ornamental copper pieces normally come with a lacquer coating to preserve the finish. Regular dusting and an occasional bath is all that is needed to keep them looking beautiful. These kinds of copper objects should never be polished.

Copper is also susceptible to bronze disease. If your copper seems as though it has bronze disease see previous tips and cures for bronze. Also, you should never use copper cooking utensils or pots as these can leach too much copper into foods and beverages, which can cause dangerous health side effects including infertility and increase chances of miscarriage. Similarly, be sure never to use steel wool, scouring pads or abrasive cleaners on copper!

TARNISH REMOVER FOR COPPER

So quick and easy you will never worry about tarnished copper pots again.

Ingredients:

> 1 **lemon or lime halved**
> **Pinch of salt**

Time to make: About 5 minutes
Storage: Single use only

Method:

Sprinkle the salt onto lemon half.

How To Use:

Rub salted lemon over copper.

Variations:

Juicy Substitute:
Substitute 1 tablespoon lemon or lime juice for fresh lemon. Pour onto salted sponge or cloth and rub copper.

Citrus Oil Substitute:
Combine 1 teaspoon orange, lemon, or lime essential oil with 2 tablespoons water. Pour on to a clean sponge that has been sprinkled with salt. Rub on copper.

OVERNIGHT TARNISH REMOVER

This recipe goes to work while you go to sleep.

Ingredients:

>   1 **cup vinegar**
>   6 **drops citrus essential oil**
>   1¼ **cups plain flour**
>   ½ **cup salt**

Yields: Approximately 3 cups

Time to make: About 5 minutes
Storage: Single use only

Method:

Combine vinegar, essential oil, flour, and salt in a medium-sized bowl. Stir to make a paste.

How To Use:

Spread onto the copper pieces you want to clean and allow to sit overnight. Rinse well under cool water and dry thoroughly. Buff with a little oil to help prevent future tarnishing.

KETCHUP TARNISH REMOVER

Tomato sauce makes a tasty red paste that will bring out the highlights in even the dullest copper.

Ingredients:

- ½ **cup tomato sauce**
- 2 **tablespoons cream of tartar**

Yields 2 ½ cups

Time to make: About 5 minutes
Storage: 2 weeks in the fridge

Method:

Combine tomato sauce and cream of tartar to make a red paste.

How To Use:

Spread onto the copper pieces you want to clean. Allow to sit for one hour. Rinse well in sudsy water and then in cool clean water. Dry with a clean soft rag.

GOLD AND SILVER

TIPS AND HINTS FOR CLEANING GOLD AND SILVER

- You should never wear rubber gloves (directly touching the metal's surface) when cleaning silver, because rubber is a natural enemy of silver. It not only encourages tarnishing but it can also actually erode the silver's finish. You can use a cotton glove on top of the rubber glove to protect you from absorbing the metal into your body.

- Never store silver in rubber containers or wrap rubber bands around it.

- Olives, eggs, salad dressing, fruit juices, vinegar, and salt should not be placed in silver containers or bowls.

- Never place flowers directly in a silver vase, as the acid released by the decaying flowers will become permanently etched in the silver. Be sure to first line your vase with glass or plastic before displaying flowers.

- Before storing silver, wrap pieces in felt (available from craft stores)

- A piece of chalk in the silver drawer will help to absorb moisture.

ROTTEN EGG CLEANER

This recipe takes its name from the smell released as the cleaner goes to work and the tarnish is removed from the silver.

Ingredients:

> 1 **tablespoon bicarbonate of soda**
> 1 **tablespoon salt**
> **Water**
> **Aluminium foil**

Yields: 2 tablespoons

Time to make: About 5 minutes
Storage: Dispose after use

Method:

Mix bicarbonate of soda and salt together.

How To Use:

Place several sheet of aluminium foil in the bottom of a container. Pour bicarbonate of soda and salt mixture over silver, then add water to cover and let stand for four to five hours. Empty out the water, rinse well under hot water, dry with a clean cloth

Note: Do not use this cleaner on items such as candle sticks that may be glued together.

PEPPERMINT POLISH

Polish silver with ease, using plain toothpaste.

Ingredient:

White toothpaste
2 or 3 drops peppermint essential oil

Time to make: About 5 minutes
Storage: Single use only

Method:

Mix toothpaste and peppermint essential oil.

How To Use:

Spread as much as you need onto a clean soft cloth. Massage silver, then rinse in hot water and dry with a soft rag.

SILVERY POLISH

This easy-to-mix formula will have your silver twinkling as brightly as the stars on a clear night.

Ingredients:

¼ cup bicarbonate of soda
Water

Yields: ¼ cup

Time to make: About 5 minutes
Storage: Dispose of any extra mixture, as it will dry out.

Method:

Put bicarbonate of soda in a small bowl; add water one tablespoon at a time and stir until you have a smooth paste.

How To Use:

Dip a clean rag into paste and rub the metal surface. Rinse well under hot water, dry with a clean cloth then polish.

Variations for the Silvery Polish

Tartar Polish:

Instead of the bicarbonate of soda, substitute 1 teaspoon cream of tartar and 1 teaspoon salt.

Silver Tarnish Remover:

Select a pot large enough to hold the pieces of gold or silver you wish to clean. Place jewellery and 3 tablespoons of cream of tartar into it and cover with water. Bring to the boil, reduce heat and simmer until tarnish is gone. Use caution, as the pieces will be hot. Allow the water and metal pieces to cool before removing. Rinse well under hot water and dry with a clean soft cloth.

GOLD AND SILVER TREASURE CLEANER

This acidic solution works well for cleaning gold and silver but it doesn't work perfectly every time. You may need to follow up with a little toothpaste to get the pieces really sparkling.

Ingredients:

Choose from one of the following ingredients.
White vinegar
Lemon juice
Lime juice
Tomato juice

Time to make: About 5 minutes
Storage: Dispose of any extra mixture, as it will dry out.

How To Use:

In a pan place the gold or silver pieces you are cleaning, pour in pure vinegar (or other ingredient of your choice to cover, and leave to stand overnight. Rinse well under hot water and dry with a clean soft cloth.

PEWTER

It is very difficult to remove tarnish from pewter and there are no natural methods that work well. However, you could try using some of the recipes for gold and silver, or this simple chalk recipe.

CLEAN WITH CABBAGE:

However, you could try using some of the recipes for gold and silver or the recipes in this section. Rubbing pewter with moist cabbage leave or freshly sliced cabbage wedges can also be effective. All worth a try!

PERFECT PEWTER POLISH

Ingredients:
> **Powdered chalk (you can use whiting or grind up a piece of chalk)**
> **Rum, brandy or vodka**

Time to make: About 5 minutes
Storage: Dispose of any extra mixture, as it will dry out.

Method:

Put chalk in a small bowl and then add the rum one tablespoon at a time, stirring until you have a smooth paste.

How To Use:

Dip a clean cloth into the paste and buff the pewter clean. Rinse in cool water and dry thoroughly.

PERFECT PEWTER PASTE

Ingredients:

> 4 **drops lavender essential oil**
> 1 **teaspoon salt**
> 1 **cup vinegar**
> **Flour to make paste**

Time to make: About 5 minutes

Storage: Dispose of any extra mixture, as it will dry out.

Method:

Add salt to vinegar and stir until dissolved, then add lavender essential oil and enough flour to make a thick paste.

How To Use:

Wearing protective gloves, rub the pewter with small circular motions. Rinse in cool water and dry well.

CAST IRON

Cast irons pans are a wonderful addition to any kitchen. They do require seasoning and special care, but if properly looked after, will last you a lifetime.

CAST IRON COOKWARE IS NATURALLY NON-STICK

THE GREAT THING ABOUT SEASONED CAST IRON COOKWARE IS THAT IT IS NATURALLY NON-STICK.

To most of us who are accustomed to the light wash n' go non-stick cookware that requires little attention (but unfortunately negatively affect your health and fertility), these heavy pans can seem old-fashioned and time consuming, yet they are intriguing. You might have inherited some already seasoned cast irons pans from your grandmother or mother, or have bought some yourself from a garage sale, and are wondering how to go about cleaning them.

CLEANING HEIRLOOM AND SEASONED CAST IRON

While the cookware is still hot, rinse it well under hot water and scrape to remove debris as needed. Never use scouring pads, steel wool or detergent on the pans, as they will release the seasoning from the pan.

NEW CAST IRON COOKWARE

New cast iron cookware is medium grey in colour; as it is used, it will naturally darken to black.

SEASONING NEW CAST IRON COOKWARE:

Pre-heat oven to 120°C

Dip a clean paper towel in lard, vegetable shortening Copha, or bacon fat and coat the entire pan.

You should never use liquid vegetable oil to coat your pan as it leaves a sticky residue and will not properly season the pan.

Bake in the oven for 15 minutes, the remove the pan and drain off any grease. Replace pan and bake for another 2 hours. It is recommended that you repeat this process a few times in order to create a stronger bond between the oil and metal surface.

Tip:

When you begin to use your pan (even though you have seasoned it) break it in by cooking foods high in fat content, such as bacon. The natural oils from these foods will create a stronger seasoning bond.

Follow this process to re-season pans whose seasoning has worn off, which have rusted, or in which food is sticking: In hot water clean the pan thoroughly using a scouring pad. Dry well (do not allow the pan to drip dry) and season again as described under Seasoning New Cast Iron Pans.

TIPS FOR STORING:

- Never let cast iron drip dry. Always dry thoroughly immediately after rinsing.

- Never store food in cast iron cookware as acids in the food will release the cookware's seasoning and give the food a metallic flavour.

- Never put cast iron pans away with the lids on. In humid weather it can cause moisture to accumulate and the pans to rust.

- You can also put a paper towel in the pan when storing to help collect moisture. If rust does develop, you should re-season the pan.

- Before putting a cast iron pan away you should wipe it again with a paper towel dipped in lard or vegetable shortening.

CHROME

CLEAN CHROME POLISH

Chrome or chromium is a steel-grey, lustrous, hard <u>metal</u> that takes a high polish and has a high melting point. It is also odourless, tasteless, and malleable. It is often used for plating items such as toasters, taps, ovens, refrigerators, golf clubs, and motor vehicles, to name just a few. If well cared for, chrome-plated pieces will last for years.

Ingredients:

> **Chrome can be safely and effectively cleaned using vinegar or soda water.**

Method:

None required

How To Use:

Moisten a soft cloth with vinegar or soda water and wipe. Dry and buff to a shine with a clean dry cloth.

EUCALYPTUS CHROME CLEANER

This is the perfect way to remove burned-on grease and foods from chrome.

Ingredients:

> **Eucalyptus essential oil**
> **Protective gloves**

Method:

None required

How To Use:

Wearing protective gloves put four to seven drops of eucalyptus oil on a clean dry cloth and rub the chrome to clean. Dry with a clean soft cloth.

RUST REMOVER

Try this recipe to remove rust stains from chrome:

Ingredients:

> 4-7 **drops Peppermint essential oil**
> 1 **tablespoon jojoba or almond oil**
> **Aluminium foil**

Method:

Set aside half the peppermint oil, combine the other half with the jojoba oil, stir.

How To Use:

First place four to seven drops of pure peppermint essential oil on a clean rag and wipe the rust spot. Using a small piece of aluminium foil, shiny side out, rub the spot, then dip a clean rag into the peppermint/jojoba oil mixture and wipe well.

TIPS TO KEEP CHROME BRIGHT AND GLEAMING:

Abrasive cleaners should never be used when caring for chrome, as they can scratch and mar the surface.

DUSTING SUPERCHARGED

Did you know that this year, on average, over 18 kilos (40 pounds) of dust will settle in your home? No wonder dusting makes homes look and feel so much better. But dusting is much more then aesthetic, it can also have a significant impact on your health; allergies to dust can lead to severe headaches and even vomiting. Much of the dust that accumulates in our homes is harmless, containing natural particles such as skin, hair, pollen, wood, natural fibres, plant matter, and paper fibres.

We have been breathing in these natural particles for thousands of years and our bodies, for the most part, have learned to tolerate them. However, modern dust contains many unhealthy pollutants such as synthetic chemicals, pesticides, paint, and other toxins. With such a broad range of dust particles in homes it is no wonder more and more people are having reactions to them, and those concerned should be tested for allergies. However, even with allergy testing and desensitising, you will still need to remove as much dust from your home as possible. The good news is that in just a few minutes a day you can easily and dramatically reduce the dust in your home.

TIPS AND HINTS FOR DUSTING:

Use a damp microfibre or cotton cloth for dusting surfaces. Dust will stick to cloth instead of being redistributed into the air and onto other surfaces.

GENERAL PURPOSE ESSENTIAL OIL DUSTER

Quick and easy to make you will really love the delicate lemon fragrance.

Ingredients:

- 2 tablespoons lemon juice
- 10 drops lemon essential oil
- 5 drops linseed or jojoba oil

Yields: 2 tablespoons

Time to make: About 5 minutes
Shelf life: A few days in the refrigerator, as lemon juice can spoil
Storage: Glass jar with a tightly-fitting lid

Method:

Combine all ingredients in a jar, secure the lid tightly and shake well.

How To Use:

Dip a clean cloth into the solution and use to dust the desired surface.

WOOD AND FURNITURE CARE AND CLEANING

DAILY WOOD CLEANER

We all have a kitchen or dining table that seems to be the centre of activities in our home and this recipe will have it sparkling clean in no time.

Ingredients:
- ¼ **cup water**
- ¼ **cup white vinegar**
- ½ **teaspoon liquid soap or dishwashing detergent**
- 3 **or 4 drops olive or jojoba oil**
- 5 **drops of your favourite essential oil**

Yields: ½ cup

Time to make: About 10 minutes
Shelf life: Indefinite
Storage: Glass jar with a tightly-fitting lid

Method:

Combine all the ingredients n a medium-sized bowl or container and stir until well mixed

How To Use:

Soak a sponge or cloth in the solution, squeeze out any excess moisture and wash surfaces.

Gabriela Rosa

Variations on the Daily Wood Cleaner

Bright as Sunshine:

To lighten wood, substitute lemon juice for vinegar in the basic recipe. The lemon juice will act as gentle bleach. Remember that lemon juice has a short shelf life so only make as much as you need.

Clean as a Whistle:

For an antiseptic cleaner add 5 to 10 drops of rosemary as your essential oil.

BOTTLED CITRUS CLEANER

The formula cannot be beaten for getting rid of dirt and grime. Before you use it, make sure your room is adequately ventilated.

Ingredients:

- 2 **cups water**
- 2 **teaspoons citrus solvent**
- 3 to 5 **drops olive or jojoba oil**

Yields: 450ml

Time to make: About 10 minutes
Shelf life: Indefinite
Storage: Spray bottle

Method:

In a spray bottle, combine water, citrus solvent, and olive oil, secure lid tightly and shake well.

How To Use:

Mist onto furniture and wipe dry with a clean soft cloth as you work. Remember to test on a small inconspicuous spot before using on the entire piece.

FURNITURE WAXES AND POLISHING CREAMS

TROPICAL POLISH

Your furniture will have a lustrous shine and a tropical twist when you use this natural wax with coconut oil.

Ingredients:

- 30 g beeswax
- 30 g carnauba wax
- 70 g jojoba or olive oil
- 40 g ounces coconut oil
- 110g distilled water
- 10 drops lemon essential oil
- ½ teaspoon grapefruit seed extract for preservative

Yields: 350ml

Time to make: About 25 minutes
Shelf life: 6 months or more
Storage: Glass jar with tightly-fitting lid

Method:

Pour distilled water into medium sized bowl, set aside. In a double boiler combine jojoba, coconut oil, beeswax and carnauba wax, melt over medium heat until mixture is smooth and the wax is completely melted. Remove from heat. Set your hand mixer on medium and slowly pour wax and oil mixture into water, beating with mixer as you combine. Add essential oils and grapefruit seed extract and beat until creamy.

How To Use:

Dip a soft cloth into the cream and massage wood. Continue to polish and buff until the cream is well worked in.

Variations on Tropical Polish:

Coca Butter:

If you love the aroma of cocoa butter you can substitute it for coconut oil in the basic recipe.

Carnauba Balm:

Use 95 gram carnauba wax and reduce beeswax to 15 gram.

Carnauba-a-coco:

Make a harder, creamier, and uniquely-scented wax by substituting both cocoa butter for coconut oil and carnauba wax for beeswax as in the above recipes.

Lovely Lavender Balm:

In addition to lemon essential oil, add 5 to 20 drops of lavender essential oil to the basic recipe.

NATURAL WAX

Nature knows best and pure natural beeswax is an excellent sealant for wood.

Ingredients:

A little bar of beeswax and a hair dryer.

How To Use:

Rub surface of wood with the bar of beeswax. Using a hair dryer (be careful not to burn the wood) heat the beeswax until it is softened and polish with a soft cloth.

FROM YOUR GARDEN WOOD CLEANER

Cleaning your wood furniture will be as enjoyable as a day in the garden with this cleaner. The geranium essential oil has a fragrance you will not find in any of the toxic commercial furniture cleaners.

Ingredients:

1 **teaspoon liquid castile soap**
5 **drops each of geranium and bergamot essential oils**
½ **cup lemon juice**

Time to make: About 5 minutes
Storage: Single use only

Method:

Combine liquid castile soap, essential oil, and lemon juice in a spray bottle, secure the lid tightly and mix well.

How To Use:

Spray directly onto the wood surface and wipe clean with a moist cloth. Follow by wiping with a soft dry cloth.

RASPBERRY WOOD CLEANER

A delightful raspberry tea for your furniture.

Ingredients:
- 1 **cup boiling water**
- 1 **tablespoon fresh raspberry leaves**
- ½ **cup lemon juice**
- ½ **cup vinegar**

Yields: 2 cups

Time to make: About 30 minutes
Shelf life: 6 months or more
Storage: Glass jar with tightly-fitting lid

Method:

Bring water to the boil, remove from heat, pour it over the raspberry leaves and allow to steep for 30 minutes. Once the raspberry tea has cooled, pour it into a spray bottle, add the lemon juice and vinegar to the spray bottle, secure the lid tightly and mix well by shaking the bottle.

How To Use:

Mist a clean soft rag with the solution and wipe wood to gently loosen and remove dirt. Moisten another rag with clean water and wipe surface to remove any residue. Finish by wiping dry with clean soft cloth.

DAILY WOOD DUSTING FORMULAE

These general-purpose formulae for use in everyday dusting are easy and quick to make. They will not only leave your wood surfaces gleaming but their fresh fragrances will leave your home smelling fabulous.

LEMON DUSTER

The fresh and delightful scent of lemon will fill your house when you use this formula. Studies show that the aroma of lemon essential oil will calm and reduce stress.

Ingredients:

    2 cups lemon balm tea
    2 drops thyme essential oil
  20 drops lemon essential oil

Yields: 450ml

Time to make: About 10 minutes
Shelf life: Indefinite
Storage: Spray bottle

Method:

Combine lemon balm tea, thyme essential oil, and lemon essential oil, in a spray bottle. Make sure the lid is tightly secured and shake well.

How To Use:

Spray wood surface and wipe clean with a soft cloth or rag.

Variation for Lemon Duster

Real Lemons:

To make using lemon juice, reduce lemon balm tea to ¼ cup and lemon essential oil to 4 drops, add ¼ cup lemon juice. Remember to store it in the refrigerator as this recipe will only last for a few days.

FROSTY WIND WOOD DUSTER

This recipe is great for any wood surface. It has a fresh cedar aroma with just a hint of sweet oranges.

Ingredients:
- ¾ **cup water**
- ½ **cup castile soap**
- 6 **drops sweet orange essential oil**
- 20 **drops cedar essential oil**

Yields: About 350ml

Time to make: About 10 minutes
Shelf life: Indefinite
Storage: Spray bottle

Method:

Combine ingredients in a spray bottle. Make sure the lid is tightly secured and shake well.

How To Use:

Spray wood surface and wipe clean with a soft cloth.

MOISTURISER FOR WOOD

The beneficial oils in this recipe will help restore and moisturise older wood pieces.

Ingredients:

4 drops lemon essential oil
2 Tablespoons natural (edible) linseed oil

Yields: 2 Tablespoons

Time to make: About 10 minutes
Shelf life: Indefinite
Storage: Small jar with tightly-fitting lid.

Method:

Combine lemon essential oil and linseed oil in a small bowl or jar (a baby food jar works well) and stir.

How To Use:

Dip a clean soft cloth into the solution and apply a very thin coat to wood, rubbing well. Finish with a clean dry cloth to remove any excess oil. Do not apply too much oil as it will attract more dust.

WOOD WAXES AND POLISHES

Whether you have a new wood piece or need to clean grandmother's dining table, the following recipes will help you care for either.

Tips and hints:

- Make extra polish or wax and store for later use; just remember to stir well before using.

- Keep an old toothbrush in or near the jar with the wax or polish to make application easier.

HERBAL OILS WOOD POLISH

Enjoy the refreshing aromatic scent of this easily-made wood polish.

Ingredients:

    4 drops lavender, rosemary, or chamomile essential oil
    ¼ cup linseed oil

Yields: ¼ cup

Time to make: About 5 minutes
Shelf life: Indefinite
Storage: Small jar with tightly-fitting lid.

Method:

Combine ingredients in a bowl or small jar and stir until blended.

How To Use:

Apply a very thin coat to wood with a toothbrush or cloth, rubbing well. Finish with a clean dry cloth to remove any excess oil. Do not apply too much oil as it will attract more dust.

WALNUT WOOD RUB

Your wood will look refreshed when you use this recipe made with three beneficial oils.

Ingredients:

    30 ml linseed oil
    30 ml walnut oil
    15 drops lemon or sweet orange essential oil

Yields: 60ml

Time to make: About 5 minutes
Shelf life: Indefinite
Storage: Small jar with tightly-fitting lid.

Method:

Combine linseed oil, walnut oil, and the citrus essential oil in a bowl or small jar and stir until blended.

How To Use:

Apply a very thin coat to the wood with a toothbrush or cloth, and massage in using smooth circular motions. Finish with a clean dry cloth to remove any excess oil. Be careful not to apply too much oil, as it will attract more dust.

CARNAUBA WOOD RENEWAL

Carnauba wax, also called the 'Queen of Waxes', is made from the leaves of the carnauba palm, a native of north-eastern Brazil. Like other oils such as almond, linseed, or walnut, it will rejuvenate and restore your wood surfaces.

Ingredients:

- 1 **cup almond, walnut, olive, or linseed oil**
- 2 **tablespoons carnauba wax flakes**
- 8 **drops lavender or rosemary essential oil**

Yields: 1 cup

Time to make: About 10 minutes
Shelf life: Indefinite
Storage: Glass or tin container with tightly-fitting lid.

Mixing:

Combine almond oil and carnauba wax in a double boiler. Bring heat up slowly and stir continuously until melted. Remove from burner and add lavender essential oil. Stir until well mixed. Pour mixture into a glass jar and allow it to cool completely before tightening the lid.

How To Use:

Apply with a cloth, massaging wax onto wood using smooth circular motions. Finish by buffing with a clean dry cloth.

BEESWAX WOOD POLISH

This is the perfect recipe for achieving a rich polish on quality, antique and heirloom wood pieces that have light finishes. Beeswax polish should never be used on painted, lacquered, or unfinished pieces. This is a little tricky to make, but worth the effort. You will need a safe, natural, citrus peel-derived turpentine alternative made by Auro Organics called 191 Plant Thinner, which can be found at most large health food stores or online at www.boostyourfertilitynow.com.

Ingredients:

2 ½	cups 191 Plant Thinner
220 g	grated beeswax
2	cups water
½	cup lemon juice
60 g	castile soap, grated
15	drops of your favourite essential oil

Yields: 5 cups

Time to make: About 30 minutes
Shelf life: Indefinite
Storage: Glass or tin container with tightly-fitting lid.

Method:

Step 1:

In a double boiler slowly melt beeswax. Remove from heat once it has completely melted and stir in Plant Thinner.

Step 2:

Combine lemon juice and water in a medium saucepan and bring to the boil. Add the castile soap and stir until it is completely melted. Remove from heat and allow to cool for five minutes.

Step 3:

Stirring constantly, pour the soap mixture into the beeswax mixture letting it very slowly cascade to the other pot in a thin stream. Stir in the essential oil and mix well. Transfer into a shallow glass or tin container and allow to cool completely before putting on the lid.

How To Use:

Apply with a cloth, massaging wax onto wood using smooth circular motions. Finish by buffing with a clean dry cloth.

FLOOR CLEANERS AND POLISH

HARDWOOD FLOOR CLEANER

A great recipe to use during busy times in your home, it easily and delightfully cleans and brightens your floors.

Ingredients:

> 2 **cups vinegar**
> 2 **cups water**
> 25 **drops peppermint essential oil**

Yields: 900 ml spray bottle

Time to make: About 5 minutes
Shelf life: Indefinite
Storage: Spray bottle

Method:

Combine vinegar, water, and peppermint essential oil in spray bottle, close lid tightly and shake until well blended.

How To Use:

Working in small sections, lightly mist with the solution and, with a sponge mop, gently wipe the floor. Follow with a dry rag or mop to absorb excess moisture.

Note: If the floorboards are warped, spray the mixture on a cloth and then wipe the floor because you don't want any water getting between the cracks and causing more warping.

CITRUS FLOOR WAX

Your floors will gleam and shine when you use this citrus-scented floor wax!

Ingredients:

- 2 **tablespoons beeswax grated**
- 2 **tablespoons carnauba wax**
- ¼ **cup lemon juice**
- 1 **cup linseed oil**
- 8 **drops lemon essential oil**
- 3 **drops sweet orange essential oil**
  Lemon juice

Yields: 1 ½ cups

Time to make: About 20 minutes
Storage: Refrigerate in a glass or tin container with a tightly-fitting lid

Method:

Combine lemon juice, linseed oil, beeswax, and carnauba wax in a double boiler. Place over low heat and stir consistently until mixture is smooth and melted. Stir in the citrus essential oil. Remove from heat and pour into a tin container (a coffee can works well) let cool until hardened.

How To Use:

Once the wax has hardened squeeze or tap the side of the can to loosen the wax from edges. Turn out the wax. Using the wax like a crayon, gently rub the floor. Soak a cloth in lemon juice and squeeze out excess liquid. Then use the cloth to massage the wax thoroughly into the floor. Finish by buffing with a clean dry cloth.

SWEET VANILLA FLOOR POLISH

Almond and walnut oil combine with vanilla extract to create a wonderful floor polish with an amazing scent.

Ingredients:

- 2 **tablespoons walnut oil**
- ¼ **cup almond oil**
- 5 **drops pure vanilla extract**

Yields: About ½ cup

Time to make: About 10 minutes
Shelf life: Indefinite
Storage: Small jar with tightly-fitting lid.

Method:

Combine walnut oil, almond oil, and vanilla extract in a small bowl and stir until well mixed.

How To Use:

Apply a small amount with a cloth to the wood surface and massage in using smooth circular motions. Finish by buffing with a clean dry cloth.

EARTHY FLOOR WAX

Try this recipe for beautiful floors that shine.

Ingredients:

- 2 tablespoons beeswax
- ¼ cup carnauba wax
- 2 cups linseed oil
- ¼ cup lemon juice
- 8 drops patchouli essential oil
- 10 drops cedar essential oil
-     Lemon juice

Yields: About ½ cup

Time to make: About 10 minutes

Storage: Refrigerate, store in a small jar with tightly-fitting lid.

Method:

In a double boiler combine carnauba wax, beeswax, linseed oil, and lemon juice. Place over low heat and stir consistently until mixture is smooth and melted. Stir in the cedar and patchouli essential oil. Remove from heat and pour into a tin container (or an old glass jar) let cool completely until hardened.

How To Use:

Once the wax has hardened, squeeze or tap the side of the can to loosen it from the edges. Turn out the wax. Using it like a crayon, gently rub the floor. Soak a cloth in lemon juice, squeeze out excess liquid and use the cloth to massage the wax thoroughly into the floor. Finish by buffing with a clean dry cloth.

REMOVER FOR WAXY BUILD-UP

This recipe is for use only on unvarnished wood floors.

Ingredients:

> 2 **cups warm vinegar**
> ½ **cup water**
> ½ **cup lemon juice**
> 1 **capful liquid castile soap**
> 10 **drops of your favourite essential oil**

Yields: About 3 cups

Time to make: About 10 minutes

Storage: Refrigerate, store in a small jar with tightly-fitting lid.

Method:

In a medium-sized bowl combine warm vinegar, water, lemon juice, castile soap, and essential oil. Stir until well mixed.

How To Use:

Moisten a sponge mop or soft bristled brush by dipping in the solution. Working in small sections gently mop floor using short back and forth strokes. Before moving to the next section follow with a dry cloth or mop.

CLEANING PAINTED WOOD FLOORS

The painted wood floor has increased in popularity lately as DIY home decorators try more new and daring ideas in their homes. This rosemary- scented floor wash will have your painted floors sparkling in no time.

Ingredients:
- 4 **litres warm water**
- 1 **cup rosemary tea***
- 2 **teaspoons washing soda**

Yields: About ½ cup

Time to make: About 10 minutes
Shelf life: Indefinite
Storage: Small jar with tightly-fitting lid.

Method:

In a large bucket, combine warm water, rosemary tea, and washing soda, stir well.

How To Use:

Saturate a sponge mop or rag in the solution and gently wash painted wood floors using a smooth back and forth motion.

*To make rosemary tea boil 1 cup water, add 2 tablespoons of fresh rosemary and remove from heat. Allow to steep for 20 to 30 minutes.

GENERAL WOOD CARE SOLUTIONS

Black Scuff Marks:

Moisten a clean soft cloth with 2 or 3 drops eucalyptus essential oil. Rub with cloth until scuff mark disappears.

Removing Burn Marks:

First check to see if the burn has made a hole in your floor. If it is only on the surface, polish it away by rubbing with a soft cloth and a thin mixture of ¼ cup rotten stone, 3 to 4 drops peppermint essential oil, and enough linseed oil to make a paste.

Removing Crayon Marks:

Apply a pea-sized amount of white toothpaste mixed with 3 to 4 drops cedar, or tea-tree essential oil to a soft cloth. Rub crayon marks until they are removed. Follow by wiping with a clean cloth dampened with vinegar. Note: Test tea-tree oil first on an inconspicuous spot for colour fastness because it may lighten dark wood.

Removing And Preventing Grease Stains On Wood Floors:

If a grease spill occurs, immediately cover it with ice cubes. The ice will harden the grease and prevent it from soaking further into the wooden floor. Scrap off any solidified grease with a blunt utensil. For unfinished wood, apply liquid castile soap and 3 to 4 drops eucalyptus oil to the spill and then blot the stain with clean white paper towels.

Removing Grease Stains From Furniture:

When the spill occurs, quickly apply salt to absorb as much of the grease as possible. Allow the salt to remain on for about an hour, and then carefully brush away the salt with a clean dry rag or vacuum. If the stain remains, try covering it with a soft cloth, set your iron on low and press (be careful not to burn the wood) lift and move the iron frequently. Replace the cloth often so any grease collected on the cloth won't be reapplied to the furniture.

Removing Scratches From Light-Coloured Wood:

Soak a soft cloth in a mixture of ½ cup olive oil and ½ cup lemon juice and gently rub the scratch.

Scratch Removal for Walnut Wood:

Rubbing a newly shelled walnut on walnut wood will help remove the scratch.

Scratch Removal for Dark Wood:

Soak a soft cloth in a solution of ½ cup vinegar and ½ cup warm water then gently rub the scratch.

Scratch Removal for Wood Floors:

Dampen very fine steel wool with natural wax floor polish (found in reputable health food stores). Rub steel wool in smooth soft circles.

Tip for Scratches:

Use a crayon of the same colour to fill a scratch if it still remains after treatment.

Removing Water Rings and Stains:

Drinks put down without coasters can leave rings and water marks. Remember to test an inconspicuous spot before you begin trying to remove the mark. Take off any previous polish by wiping with a rag moistened with vinegar. Dry thoroughly with a clean soft cloth. Working from the outside of the water stain in, apply linseed oil or mayonnaise. Allow to stand for a few hours then polish with a clean soft cloth. You might also try 2 to 4 drops of peppermint essential oil. If the stain has penetrated, try using your fingers to rub toothpaste, bicarbonate of soda, or pulverized chalk into it.

Note: If using chalk, use a colour that closely matches the colour of the wood you are restoring.

Removing Candle Wax from Wood:

Use a hairdryer to heat the wax. Be careful not to scorch the wood. As the wax softens and melts, dab clean with a rag.

LEATHER CLEANERS FOR FURNITURE

LEATHER BALM

A creamy, moisturising leather rejuvenator.

Ingredients:

- 1 **cup walnut oil**
- ½ **cup water**
- ½ **cup glycerine**
- 30 **g beeswax**
- 4 **capsules vitamin E**
- 3 **drops essential oil of lavender**

Yields: About 450ml

Time to make: about 25 minutes
Shelf life: About 6 months
Storage: Keep in a cool dark place in a glass jar with a tightly-fitting lid

Method:

In a double boiler combine beeswax and walnut oil and melt over a medium heat. Once mixture is smooth and completely melted, remove from heat and stir in water, lavender essential oil and glycerine. Break open vitamin E capsules and empty contents into mixture. With an electric hand mixer, beat until creamy.

How To Use:

Gently massage into leather. Finish by wiping with a clean soft cloth.

JOJOBA LEATHER MOISTURISER

The vinegar will clean while the jojoba oil moisturises.

Ingredients:

½ **cup vinegar**

5 **drops jojoba oil**

Yields: About ½ cup

Time to make: About 5 minutes

Shelf life: Indefinite

Storage: Glass jar with a tightly-fitting lid

Method:

In a small bowl combine vinegar and jojoba oil. Mix well.

How To Use:

Soak a cloth in the solution, and then wipe the leather.

LEATHER BATH

This no-need-to-rinse, easy-to-make formula is also a wonderful disinfectant.

Ingredients:

- ¼ **cup water**
- ¼ **cup vinegar**
- ¼ **cup vodka**
- 5 **drops olive or jojoba oil**

Yields: About ¾ cup

Time to make: About 10 minutes
Shelf life: Indefinite
Storage: Glass jar with tightly-fitting lid

Method:

In a glass jar combine water, vinegar, vodka, and oil. Secure the lid tightly and shake well.

How To Use:

Moisten a soft cloth in the solution and rub leather. Follow with lanoline or leather balm.

LEATHER SPOT REMOVER

This method requires only egg white. Tailor the amount of egg white to the size of the spot you wish to remove.

Ingredients:

> **Egg whites**

Time to make: A couple of minutes
Shelf life: About 2 hours
Storage: Discard after use

Method:

In a medium-sized bowl beat egg white with an electric hand mixer until stiff.

How To Use:

Scoop a small amount on to a clean rag and gently rub the spot. Allow to stand. Finish by wiping clean with warm water.

SADDLE SOAP ALTERNATIVE POLISH

Like saddle soap this recipe cleans and moisturises.

Ingredients:

> ½ **teaspoon liquid castile soap**
> ½ **cup jojoba oil**

Yields: About1/2 cup

Time to make: About 5 minutes
Shelf life: Indefinite
Storage: Glass jar with tightly-fitting lid

Method:

In a small bowl, combine soap and jojoba oil. Using a whisk, blend well.

How To Use:

Moisten a soft cloth in the solution and rub leather. Wipe off any residue with a clean dry towel. There is no need to rinse.

GREASE STAIN REMOVER

Glycerine cleans and it will also help seal moisture into your leather and keep it from drying out. You will need about a teaspoon of glycerine, depending on the size of the stain.

How To Use:

Cover the stain with glycerine and allow it to soak for about 10 minutes. Use a soft cloth to wipe up the glycerine. Finish by washing away residue with warm sudsy water.

SMALL SPILL CORNMEAL ABSORBER

Cornmeal works well to absorb some stains. The size of the spill will determine how much cornmeal you need.

How To Use:

Pour cornmeal on to a damp, soft cloth and dab stain. Allow to dry thoroughly. Brush the cornmeal away.

LANOLIN

Lanolin is oil extracted from sheep's wool. It is sometimes used as a base in ointments and salves for human skin. No wonder it works so well for moisturising leather.

How To Use:

Squeeze a small amount onto a rag and massage into the leather. Finish by buffing with a soft cloth.

SADDLE SOAP

An old time favourite for cleaning, softening, and preserving leather.

Ingredients:

- 2 **tablespoons each jojoba and olive oil**
- 28 **gram beeswax**
- 2 **tablespoons liquid castile soap**
- 6 **tablespoons water**
- 2 **tablespoons vodka or rum**

Yields: About 1 cup

Time to make: About 30 minutes

Shelf life: At least 6 months

Storage: Keep in a cool dry place in a glass or tin container with a tightly-fitting lid

Method:

Melt jojoba oil, olive oil, beeswax and liquid castile soap over a medium heat. When the beeswax is completely melted, remove from heat and add water and vodka. Immediately beat with an electric hand mixer until well blended.

How To Use:

Dip a damp cloth into the saddle soap and work up lather. Apply this to the leather in small circles. Finish by removing any build-up with a damp cloth, residue from the soap can damage the leather. Wipe leather dry with a clean soft cloth.

Air Fresheners

Air Fresheners

The Air We Breathe

The air inside your home is likely to have more contaminants and pollution than the air on a major city street. Studies have found that the air inside an average home has pollution levels two to five times higher than the outside air and it can be as much as one hundred times higher. Studies have also found that indoor air contaminates number around 900. The Consumer Product Safety Commission discovered during one study that samples from outdoor testing locations contained less than 10 volatile organic compounds (VOCs) while indoor samples contained 150 of these airborne chemical toxins.

"As a direct result of higher exposure to toxic chemicals in common household products women who work at home have a 54% higher death rate from cancer than those who work away from home."

—Toronto Indoor Air Conference 1990

So, what is the main cause of indoor air contamination? The chemical products we use to clean and freshen our homes—toxins and pollutants that can have a damaging effect on our health and fertility. Obviously it is impossible to eliminate all airborne toxins but there are ways we can reduce their impact. For example, using commercial air fresheners actually contaminates the air instead of cleaning it. They may leave a lingering fresh scent, but what else do they leave lingering in your indoor space? That synthetic fragrances, comes with PCBs, naphthalene, formaldehyde, sodium bisulphate, glycol ethers, alcohols, propellants, and many other volatile organic compounds. These chemicals can cause reproductive and developmental disorders as wells as allergic reactions ranging from watery eyes and stuffy noses to severe asthma attacks.

Tips and Hints:

- The simplest way to help reduce the toxins from your home is to open the windows, allowing fresh air to circulate;

- Pour ½ cup vinegar in bowl or jar. Set open jar near where the odour you want removed;

- Striking a match or a lighter will neutralised any odours in the bathroom;

- Burning 100% pure essential oils in a little water, in an oil burner will beautifully fragrance your home.

Plants: The Best Air Purifiers

Plants are a beautiful and natural way to purify indoor air. NASA studies have shown that ordinary houseplants will help reduce the amount of toxins and create clean, healthy air. Experts recommend you have 1 plant for every 11 square metres of indoor space, the more plants you have the cleaner and healthier your air will be.

Another very important benefit of plants is that they help to diminish the damaging effects of electromagnetic radiation on body cells, particularly gametes such as the female egg and sperm and DNA. So the more plants you have around, the better! For more information see The Natural Fertility Solution Take-Home Program available at www. boostyourfertilitynow.com.

WHICH PLANTS SHOULD YOU GROW?

This is a list of plants with the best air purifying capabilities.

ALL-PURPOSE AIR PURIFIERS

These plants are the best general-purpose air purifiers for your home and office:

- Boston Fern (Nephrolepis exaltata bostoniensis)

- Areca Palm (Chyrsalidocarpus lutescens)

- Lady Palm (Rhapis excelsa)

- Bamboo Palm (Chamaedorea seifrizii)

- Golden Pothos (Epipremnum aureum)

- Peace Lily (Spathiphyllum sp.)

- Kimberly Queen Fern (Nephrolepis obliterata)

- Gerbera Daisy (Gerbera jamesonii)

- Spider Plant (Chlorophytum comosum)

- Schefflera (Brassaia actinophylla)

- Dracaena Warneckei (Dracaena deremensis warneckei)

- Weeping Fig (Ficus benjamina 'Contorta' or Ficus benjamina 'Pandora')

FORMALDEHYDE REMOVERS

These plants have been found to work especially well for removing formaldehyde from your immediate home and office environment:

- Rubber Plant (Ficus robusta)

- Dracaena Janet Craig (Dracaena deremensis)

- English Ivy (Hedera helix)

- Corn Plant (Bracaena fragrans Massangeana)

- Ficus Alii (Ficus macleilandii alii)

- Chrysanthemum (Chrysanthemum morifolium)

XYLENE REMOVERS

These plants are noted for their ability to remove xylene from your immediate home and office environment:

- Dwarf Date Palm (Phoenix roebelenii)

- Dragon Tree (Dracaena marginata)

RECIPES FOR CLEANER AIR

CLEAN NATURALLY AIR FRESHENER

This freshener doesn't mask odours it absorbs them. It works well for every room of the house. You will be surprised how well it gets rid of even odorous kitchen smells like onion and garlic.

Ingredients:

>1 cup white distilled vinegar
>25 drops lavender essential oil or your favourite scent

Yields: 1 cup

Time to make: About 5 minutes
Shelf life: Indefinite
Storage: Fine-Mist Spray bottle

Method:

Combine vinegar, and essential oil in a fine-mist-spray bottle (you can usually find a fine-mist spray bottle at a beauty supply story). Secure lid tightly and shake well.

How To Use:

Shake well before each use. Mist into air where ever there is an unpleasant odour.

Note: Don't put your face into the mist. Vinegar can irritate eyes.

FRESH SCENTS

Ever wonder what to do with those pretty trinket boxes? Here's a way to display your beautiful treasures while freshening the air.

Ingredients:

>   1   **cup of Bicarbonate Soda**
> 10-15   **drops of your favourite essential oil**

Yields: 1 cup

Time to make: About 5 minutes
Shelf life: Indefinite, replace when essential oil small finishes
Storage: Display box

Method:

Add 10 to 15 drops of your favourite essential oil into the one cup of bicarbonate soda and mix well.

How To Use:

Place box in an area where you will enjoy the scent or a room that needs particular attention, such as a bathroom or the kitchen. The bicarbonate of soda will deodorise while the essential oil will perfume the air. Over time the essential oil will evaporate, so add a boost whenever it is needed by reapplying the essential oil.

In a couple of months the bicarbonate of soda will have finished deodorising. Pour it down the drain and add a little vinegar, which will make the bicarbonate of soda fizz. Allow it to stand for 20 minutes and then rinse the drain thoroughly by running hot water. This will help keep your drains fresh and clog free.

LEMON GARBAGE DEODORISER

Try this idea to rid the kitchen of that old garbage smell. You can mix it up in the same box the bicarbonate of soda comes in.

Ingredients:

One 1 kg box of bicarbonate soda
1 teaspoon lemon essential oil

Yields: 4 cups

Time to make: About 5 minutes
Shelf life: Indefinite
Storage: Bicarbonate of soda box, taped closed

Method:

Use a fork to make a few small holes near the centre of the box of bicarbonate of soda. Pour the essential oil into the holes. Mix with the fork, first from one side and then the other. Reseal with tape.

How To Use:

Pour ¼ cup into the bottom of your kitchen rubbish bin. Leave it there and replace with a fresh rubbish bag. It will help keep your bin mildew-free, and dry. And the next time you clean your bin, it will make a nice paste to scrub with.

Replace the bicarbonate soda mix as required.

ELEMENTAL REMEDY

Here's an idea to keep your kitchen disposal clean and odour free.

Ingredients:

> ½ **cup orange, lemon, lime, or grapefruit rind**
> 1 **cup ice cubes**

Yields: 1 ½ cups

Time to make: About 5 minutes
Shelf life: Single use only

Method:

Mix ice and citrus rind together into your kitchen disposal unit.

How To Use:

Turn on kitchen disposal unit and wait while the ice cubes scrub out dirt and grease and the citrus acid from the rinds clean.

Note: While the ice cubes are ground up it will be quite noisy.

VERY VANILLA AIR REFRESHER

So simple and it smells so good! It works especially well in closets, cars, and bathrooms.

Ingredients:

Natural vanilla extract, enough to saturate cotton ball
Cotton ball
Small glass jar

Yields: 1 freshener

Time to make: About 5 minutes
Shelf life: Replace when smell completely dissipates
Storage: Glass jar

Method:

Saturate cotton ball with natural vanilla extract and place into a small glass jar with a whole on the top.

How To Use:

Place the jar in an area you would like to freshen. It needs replacing when it has dried out.

POMANDERS

These date back to the 16th century. They are fun to create, and make great gifts.

Ingredients:

> 1 **orange**
> 1 **bottle of whole cloves**
> **Ribbon**

Yields: 1 freshener

Time to make: About 30 minutes
Shelf life: Indefinite
Storage: Hang in the closet

How to make:

Push the whole cloves into the rind of the orange in decorative patterns. Then tie a ribbon around the orange and hang in a closet.

TOILET BOWL FRESHENER

Use this simple formula to freshen your toilet bowl. If you want to save water, this will keep your toilet bowl fresh between flushings.

Ingredients:

> **6 or 7 drops peppermint essential oil**
> **2 cups vinegar**

Yields: 2 cups

Time to make: About 5 minutes
Shelf life: Indefinite
Storage: Glass jar with a tightly-fitting lid.

Method:

Combine vinegar and essential oil in a glass jar. Secure lid and shake well.

How To Use:

Pour 1 cup into toilet bowl. Allow to stand an hour or until your next flushing.

KITTY LITTER FRESHENER

Try this recipe for a fresh and clean smelling litter box. Always wear a mask and disposable gloves when handling kitty litter. Women should avoid this completely as toxoplasmosis (a common parasite found in kitty litters) can cause miscarriages and fertility problems.

Ingredients:

2   cups bicarbonate of soda
24 drops eucalyptus or peppermint essential oil

Yields: 2 cups

Time to make: About 5 minutes
Shelf life: Indefinite
Storage: Glass jar with a tightly-fitting lid.

Method:

Combine bicarbonate of soda and essential oil in a glass jar, shake to mix.

How To Use:

Pour about half of the litter freshener into the bottom of the litter pan then add litter.

Gabriela Rosa

Potpourri

Potpourri is a collection of dried flower petals, leaves, herbs, and spices. There are so many combinations to try so experiment and find a fragrance that really expresses who you are. There are so many uses for potpourris, put them in sachets or pillows, or in an open vase or box. Here are some ideas to inspire.

EARLY AUTUMN HARVEST

A sweet mixture as fresh as autumn fields!

Ingredients:

- ½ cup chamomile
- ½ cup purple basil
- ½ cup marjoram
- ¼ cup white or yellow yarrow
- ¼ cup juniper berries
- ¼ cup oakmoss
- 2 tablespoons mace
- 1 teaspoon orange peel
- 10 drops cedar essential oil

Yields: 2 ½ cups

Time to make: About 20 minutes
Shelf life: Indefinite
Storage: Display container.

Method:

Combine all the ingredients in a glass container. Stir with a spoon until mixed. Gently shake the potpourri once a day for 1 to 2 months or until you feel the fragrance is full and rich.

How To Use:

Fill sachets and pillows, or display in a vase or box.

SIMPLY ROMANTIC

This elegant fragrance will enrich your home.

Ingredients:

- 1 **cup lavender buds**
- 1 **cup rose petals**
- 1 **cup rose geranium leaves**
- ½ **cup lemon verbena leaves**
- 8 **drops sandalwood essential oil**

Yields: 3 ½ cups

Time to make: About 20 minutes
Shelf life: Indefinite
Storage: Glass jar or display container.

Method:

Combine all the ingredients in a glass container. Stir with a spoon until mixed. Gently shake the potpourri once a day for 1 to 2 months or until you feel the fragrance is full and rich.

How To Use:

You can place this blend in a pot of water and simmer for a vaporised air-freshener, or fill sachets and pillows, or display in a vase or box.

SEA BREEZE

This will remind you of cool saltwater mists.

Ingredients:

- ½ **cup torn eucalyptus leaves,**
- ½ **cup peppermint leaves**
- ½ **cup rosemary leaves**
- ¼ **cup thyme leaves**
- ¼ **cup whole cloves**
- 2 **teaspoons lemon rind, grated**

Yields: 2 cups

Time to make: About 20 minutes
Shelf life: Indefinite
Storage: Glass jar or display container.

Method:

Combine all the ingredients in a glass container. Stir with a spoon until mixed. Gently shake the potpourri once a day for 1 to 2 months or until you feel the fragrance is full and rich.

How To Use:

You can place this blend in a pot of water and simmer for a vaporised air-freshener, or fill sachets, and pillows, or display in a vase or box.

GARDEN DELIGHTS

Brimming with flowers, this fragrance is sweet and simple.

Ingredients:

- 1 **cup statice**
- 1 **cup cornflowers**
- 1 **cup snapdragons**
- ½ **cup rose petals**
- ½ **cup marigolds**
- ½ **cup sunflower petals**
- ½ **cup rose hips**
- ¼ **cup ground anise**
- 2 **crushed cinnamon sticks**

Yields: 5 ½ cups

Time to make: About 20 minutes

Shelf life: Indefinite

Storage: Glass jar or display container.

Method:

Combine all the ingredients in a glass container. Stir with a spoon until mixed. Gently shake the potpourri once a day for 1 to 2 months or until you feel the fragrance is full and rich.

How To Use:

Fill sachets and pillows, or display in a vase or box.

AFTERNOON WALK

This delightful aroma is charming and earthy.

Ingredients:

    1 **cup bay leaves**
    1 **cup sage**
    2 **cups dried apples**
  ½ **cup whole cloves**
    4 **cinnamon sticks snapped in half**

Yields: 4 ½ cups

Time to make: About 20 minutes
Shelf life: Indefinite
Storage: Glass jar or display container.

Method:

Combine all the ingredients in a glass container. Stir with a spoon until mixed. Gently shake the potpourri once a day for 1 to 2 months or until you feel the fragrance is full and rich.

How To Use:

You can place this blend in a pot of water and simmer for a vaporised air-freshener, or fill sachets and pillows, or display in a vase or box.

ORANGE BOUQUET

A lovely orange fragrance.

Ingredients:

- 2 **cups sliced orange rind**
- 1 **cup sliced dried apple**
- 1 **cup marigold blossoms**
- ½ **cup whole cloves**
- 10 **drops sweet orange essential oil**

Yields: 4 ½ cups

Time to make: About 20 minutes

Shelf life: Indefinite

Storage: Glass jar with lid or display container, keep in a cool dry place, away from direct sun light.

Method:

Combine all the ingredients in a glass container. Stir with a spoon until mixed. Gently shake the potpourri once a day for 1 to 2 months or until you feel the fragrance is full and rich.

How To Use:

You can place this blend in a pot of water and simmer for a vaporised air-freshener, or fill sachets and pillows, or display in a vase or box.

GARDEN FRAGRANCES

This beautiful perfume will transform your home into a summer garden.

Ingredients:

> 1 **cup rose hips**
> 1 **cup magnolia flowers**
> 1 **cup bee balm blossoms**
> 1 **cup lemon verbena**
> ½ **cup calendula flowers**

Yields: 5 cups

Time to make: About 20 minutes

Shelf life: Indefinite

Storage: Glass jar with lid or display container, keep in a cool dry place, away from direct sun light.

Method:

Combine all the ingredients in a glass container. Stir with a spoon until mixed. Gently shake the potpourri once a day for 1 to 2 months or until you feel the fragrance is full and rich.

How To Use:

Fill sachets, and pillows, or display in a vase or box.

FIELDS OF FLOWERS

Sweet as an island breeze, this lavender scent will calm and relax.

Ingredients:

- ¼ **cup lavender**
- ¼ **cup verbena**
- ¼ **cup sweet woodruff**
- ½ **cup jasmine flowers**
- 2 **teaspoons coriander peel**
- 1 **teaspoons gingerroot**

Yields: 4 ½ cups

Time to make: About 20 minutes

Shelf life: Indefinite

Storage: Glass jar with lid or display container, keep in a cool dry place, away from direct sun light.

Method:

Combine all the ingredients in a glass container. Stir with a spoon until mixed. Gently shake the potpourri once a day for 1 to 2 months or until you feel the fragrance is full and rich.

How To Use:

Fill sachets, and pillows, or display in a vase or box.

VANILLA AND FLOWERS

This dreamy fragrance will remind you of summer rain.

Ingredients:

- 1 **cup lemon verbena leaves**
- 1 **cup jasmine flowers**
- ½ **cup ginger root minced**
- 1 **vanilla bean, sliced in small pieces**
- 2 **Tonka beans (Tonka beans maybe found at natural food stores. A member of the pea family they have a scent reminiscent of vanilla beans)**
- 1 **tablespoon sandalwood chips**
- 20 **drops patchouli essential oil**

Yields: 2 ½ cups

Time to make: About 20 minutes

Shelf life: Indefinite

Storage: Glass jar with lid or display container, keep in a cool dry place, away from direct sun light.

Method:

Combine all the ingredients in a glass container. Stir with a spoon until mixed. Gently shake the potpourri once a day for 1 to 2 months or until you feel the fragrance is full and rich.

How To Use:

Fill sachets, and pillows, or display in a vase or box.

FROM THE FOREST

A crisp, engaging blend.

Ingredients:

> 1 **cup empress red nasturtium flowers**
> 1 **cup whole sage leaves**
> 1 **cup evening primrose flowers**
> ½ **cup clary sage leaves**
> ½ **cup oakmoss**
> ¼ **cup chopped angelica root**
> 25 **drops patchouli essential oil**

Yields: 4 ½ cups

Time to make: About 20 minutes

Shelf life: Indefinite

Storage: Glass jar with lid or display container, keep in a cool dry place, away from direct sun light.

Method:

Combine all the ingredients in a glass container. Stir with a spoon until mixed. Gently shake the potpourri once a day for 1 to 2 months or until you feel the fragrance is full and rich.

How To Use:

You can place this blend in a pot of water and simmer for a vaporised air-freshener, or fill sachets, pillows, or display in a vase or box.

SWEET CITRUS SUNRISE

A light and refreshing fragrance blend.

Ingredients:

1	**cup marigold blossoms**
1	**cup peppermint leaves**
1	**cup lemon balm leaves and blossoms**
½	**cup chamomile blossoms**
½	**cup lemon thyme leaves**
¼	**cup orange peel grated**
¼	**cup lemon peel grated**
2	**tablespoon coriander**
15	**drops bergamot essential oil**

Yields: 4 ½ cups

Time to make: About 20 minutes

Shelf life: Indefinite

Storage: Glass jar with lid or display container, keep in a cool dry place, away from direct sun light.

Method:

Combine all the ingredients in a glass container. Stir with a spoon until mixed. Gently shake the potpourri once a day for 1 to 2 months or until you feel the fragrance is full and rich.

How To Use:

Fill sachets, and pillows, or display in a vase or box.

BUTTERFLY BLEND

This scent is made from flowers often frequented by butterflies.

Ingredients:

- ½ **cup chamomile blossoms**
- ½ **cup dill stems, leaves, and blossoms**
- ½ **cup sweet clover blossoms**
- ½ **cup lavender blossoms**
- ¼ **cup lemongrass**

Yields: 2 ½ cups

Time to make: About 20 minutes

Shelf life: Indefinite

Storage: Glass jar with lid or display container, keep in a cool dry place, away from direct sun light.

Method:

Combine all the ingredients in a glass container. Stir with a spoon until mixed. Gently shake the potpourri once a day for 1 to 2 months or until you feel the fragrance is full and rich.

How To Use:

Fill sachets, and pillows, or display in a vase or box.

FIELDS AND FOREST BLEND

This festive potpourri will add a wonderful fragrance, perfect for winter entertaining.

Ingredients:

- 1 **cup evergreen pine needles**
- ½ **cup dried apples diced**
- ½ **cup cinnamon sticks, snapped into small pieces**
- ½ **cup cedar chips**
- ¼ **cup whole cloves**
- 1 **tablespoon mace**
- 1 **tablespoon allspice berries**
- 1 **tablespoon ginger root chopped**
- 1 **tablespoon ground cinnamon**
- 10 **drops myrrh essential oil**
- 15 **drops frankincense essential oil**

Yields: 3 ½ cups

Time to make: About 20 minutes

Shelf life: Indefinite

Storage: Glass jar with lid or display container, keep in a cool dry place, away from direct sun light.

Method:

Combine all the ingredients in a glass container. Stir with a spoon until mixed. Gently shake the potpourri once a day for 1 to 2 months or until you feel the fragrance is full and rich.

How To Use:

You can place this blend in a pot of water and simmer for a vaporised air-freshener, or fill sachets or pillows, or display in a vase or box.

Gabriela Rosa

Herbal Air Sprays

Herbal sprays are simple to make. They bring a light refreshing fragrance to your living spaces while eliminating unpleasant odours. They can also uplift your spirits through their refreshing scents. Keep one in the kitchen, bathroom, and bedroom, so you can mist whenever needed.

THYME ON THE WATERS

This recipe is the perfect kitchen odour eliminator. It not only works well for deodorising but it also works as a vegetable and fruit wash.

Ingredients:

> 1 **cup distilled water**
> 6 **drops thyme essential oil**

Yields: 1 cup

Time to make: About 5 minutes
Shelf life: Indefinite
Storage: Spray bottle

Method:

Wash spray bottle well, combine water and essential oil in bottle. Secure lid and shake well.

How To Use:

Shake before each use. Mist into air for a fresh scent. To use as a fruit and vegetable wash: Mist produce with the solution and scrub gently using a vegetable brush. Rinse well under cool water.

KITCHEN SPICE BLEND

A fun blend of spices that creates a fresh baked cookie aroma.

Ingredients:

- **1 cup distilled water**
- **2 drops cinnamon essential oil**
- **2 drops ginger essential oil**
- **2 drops vanilla essential oil**

Yields: 1 cup

Time to make: About 5 minutes

Shelf life: Indefinite

Storage: Spray bottle

Method:

Wash spray bottle well and combine the water and essential oils in the bottle. Secure lid and shake well.

How To Use:

Shake before each use. Mist into the air for a fresh scent.

LOVELY HERB BLEND

A delicate and romantic herb blend.

Ingredients:

- 3 drops lavender essential oil
- 2 drops rose essential oil
- 1 drop geranium essential oil
- 1 drop rosemary essential oil
- 1 drop sweet orange essential oil

Yields: 1 cup

Time to make: About 5 minutes
Shelf life: Indefinite
Storage: Spray bottle

Method:

Wash spray bottle well and combine the water and essential oils in the bottle. Secure lid and shake well.

How To Use:

Shake before each use. Mist into the air for a fresh scent.

EARTH AND SKY BLEND

Ingredients:

- 1 **cup distilled water**
- 2 **drops sage essential oil**
- 2 **drops thyme essential oil**
- 1 **drop cedar essential oil**
- 1 **drop patchouli essential oil**
- 1 **drop frankincense essential oil**

Yields: 1 cup

Time to make: About 5 minutes
Shelf life: Indefinite
Storage: Spray bottle

Method:

Wash spray bottle well and combine the water and essential oils in the bottle. Secure lid and shake well.

How To Use:

Shake before each use. Mist into the air for a fresh scent.

RARE SCENT BLEND

Ingredients:

- 1 **cup distilled water**
- 2 **drops vanilla essential oil**
- 2 **drops jasmine**
- 1 **drop sandalwood essential oil**
- 1 **drop ylang-ylang essential oil**
- 1 **drop neroli essential oil**
- 1 **drop rose essential oil**

Yields: 1 cup

Time to make: About 5 minutes
Shelf life: Indefinite
Storage: Spray bottle

Method:

Wash spray bottle well and combine the water and essential oils in the bottle. Secure lid and shake well.

How To Use:

Shake before each use. Mist into the air for a fresh scent.

FAR EAST BLEND

The scent of the Orient.

Ingredients:

- 1 **cup distilled water**
- 1 **drop patchouli essential oil**
- 1 **drop sandalwood essential oil**
- 1 **drop cedar essential oil**
- 1 **drop lime essential oil**
- 1 **drop coriander essential oil**

Yields: 1 cup

Time to make: About 5 minutes

Shelf life: Indefinite

Storage: Spray bottle

Method:

Wash spray bottle well and combine the water and essential oils in the bottle. Secure lid and shake well.

How To Use:

Shake before each use. Mist into the air for a fresh scent.

RENEWING BLEND

Ingredients:

- 1 **cup distilled water**
- 2 **drops lavender essential oil**
- 2 **drops basil essential oil**
- 1 **drop orange essential oil**
- 1 **drop peppermint essential oil**
- 1 **drop nutmeg essential oil**

Yields: 1 cup

Time to make: About 5 minutes
Shelf life: Indefinite
Storage: Spray bottle

Method:

Wash spray bottle well and combine the water and essential oils in the bottle. Secure lid and shake well.

How To Use:

Shake before each use. Mist into the air for a fresh scent.

Gabriela Rosa

NO-STRESS BLEND

Keep a bottle of this blend at your office to calm your spirits on stressful days.

Ingredients:

- 1 **cup distilled water**
- 2 **drops chamomile essential oil**
- 1 **drop clary sage essential oil**
- 1 **drop bergamot essential oil**
- 1 **drop yarrow essential oil**

Yields: 1 cup

Time to make: About 5 minutes
Shelf life: Indefinite
Storage: Spray bottle

Method:

Wash spray bottle well and combine the water and essential oils in the bottle. Secure lid and shake well.

How To Use:

Shake before each use. Mist into the air for a fresh scent.

SPRING BLEND

The fresh scent of spring blooms.

Ingredients:

- 1 **cup distilled water**
- 2 **drops lemon essential oil**
- 2 **drops orange essential oil**
- 2 **drops thyme essential oil**
- 1 **drop basil essential oil**

Yields: 1 cup

Time to make: About 5 minutes
Shelf life: Indefinite
Storage: Spray bottle

Method:

Wash spray bottle well and combine the water and essential oils in the bottle. Secure lid and shake well.

How To Use:

Shake before each use. Mist into the air for a fresh scent.

Gabriela Rosa

Sachets

Fill a small handmade bag or even an old sock with dried herbs, flowers and essential oil and you have a simple to make air fresher with many uses. Tie a ribbon around the sachet and hang it in a wardrobe to give clothes a light fragrance, or tuck a sweetly scented sachet into your lingerie drawer, or any other drawer. It will help keep bugs away while keeping your clothes and linens smelling fresh.

Tip: Put a sachet in regularly worn shoes to keep them smelling fresh.

LINEN FRESHENER

Adds a lovely fragrance to towels and linens.

Ingredients:

- 4 **cups oak moss**
- 2 **cups lavender blossoms and leaves**
- 2 **cups rosemary leaves**
- ½ **cup lemon verbena**
- 1 **tablespoon orrisroot**
- 8 **drops lavender essential oil**
- 5 **drops rosemary essential oil**

Yields: 4 to 6 sachets

Time to make: About 15 minutes
Shelf life: Indefinite
Storage: Sachets

Method:

Combine the moss and herbs in a glass bowl. Stir in orrisroot with a wooden spoon. Add essential oils of lavender and rosemary and stir well.

How To Use:

Spoon into a small bag, a wedding favour bag works well, or you can make your own by sewing a small square from cotton cloth. Leave one side open so you can spoon in the dried herbal mixture. Once the bag is filled, sew the edge closed or pull closed the draw string. Tuck into a drawer or hang in a closet or cupboard.

Note: Make sure all of your herbs are thoroughly dried before you fill the sachet.

PEPPER AND SPICE

This fresh and zesty blend has a wonderful fragrance for the holidays. Sachets also make nice gifts.

Ingredients:

>   2 **cups cinnamon chips**
> ½ **cup peppercorns**
> ½ **cup whole cloves**
> ½ **cup gingerroot, sliced**
>   2 **tablespoons ground cinnamon**
>   1 **tablespoon aniseed**
>   2 **tablespoons caraway seed**

Yields: 2 to 4 sachets

Time to make: About 10 minutes
Shelf life: Indefinite
Storage: Sachets

Method:

Combine spices in a glass bowl and mix well using your hands or a spoon.

How To Use:

Spoon into a small bag, a wedding favour bag works well, or you can make your own sachet by sewing a small square from cotton cloth. Leave one side open so you can spoon in the dried herbal mixture. Once the bag is filled, sew the edge closed or pull closed the draw string. Tuck into a drawer or hang in a closet or cupboard.

Note: Make sure all of your herbs are thoroughly dried before you fill the sachet.

WARDROBE FRESHENER

Try this blend for a long-lasting scent in sock or lingerie drawers

Ingredients:

- 2 **cups oak moss**
- 3 **cups cedar chips**
- 1 **cup sandalwood chips**
- 1 **cup dried sage**
- 1 **vanilla bean, crushed**
- 14 **drops patchouli essential oil**

Yields: 4 to 6 sachets

Time to make: About 15 minutes
Shelf life: Indefinite
Storage: Sachets

Method:

Combine moss, cedar, sandalwood, and sage in a glass bowl. Blend together using a wooden spoon. Add essential oil of patchouli and crushed vanilla bean. Stir until well mixed.

How To Use:

Spoon into a small bag, a wedding favour bag works well, or you can make your own sachet by sewing a small square from cotton cloth. Leave one side open so you can spoon in the dried herbal mixture. Once the bag is filled, sew the edge closed or pull closed the draw string. Tuck into a drawer or hang in a closet or cupboard.

Note: Make sure all of your herbs are thoroughly dried before you fill the sachet.

ODOUR REMOVER FOR SHOES

Place socks filled with this blend into smelly shoes to remove odours.

Ingredients:

2	**cups dried sage**
2	**cups cedar chips**
1 ½	**cups dried lemon balm**
½	**cup bicarbonate of soda**
2	**tablespoons range pea, grated**
8	**drops lemon essential oil**
10	**drops rosemary essential oil**

Yields: 4 to 6 sachets

Time to make: About 15 minutes
Shelf life: Indefinite
Storage: Sachets

Method:

Combine cedar, bicarbonate of soda, grated orange peel and herbs in a glass bowl. Blend together using a wooden spoon. Add essential oils and stir well.

How To Use:

Divide the mixture between two clean (old) socks and tie a knot in the open end. Stuff one sock into each shoe and leave overnight. Put the socks back into the shoes whenever they are not in use.

SHOE ODOUR ABSORBER

Make your tennis shoes smell fresher.

Ingredients:

- 1 **cup bicarbonate of soda**
- 1 **cup calendula flowers**
- 1 **cup peppermint leaves**
- 2 **cups natural clay cat litter**
- 10 **drops wintergreen essential oil**
- 10 **drops eucalyptus essential oil**
- 10 **drops peppermint essential oil**

Yields: 2 to 4 sachets

Time to make: About 15 minutes
Shelf life: Indefinite
Storage: Sachets

Method:

Combine cat litter and bicarbonate of soda in a glass bowl. Mix well using a wooden spoon. Add herbs and stir, and then add essential oils. Stir again until well blended.

How To Use:

Divide the mixture between two clean (old) socks, and tie a knot in the open end. Stuff one sock into each shoe and leave overnight. Put the socks back into the shoes whenever they are not in use.

AIR FRESHENER TIPS AND HINTS:

Medieval Herb Room Freshener:

Tie ribbon around dry herbs and hang in your kitchen. Try rosemary, lavender, sage, lemongrass, citronella, or mint.

Firewood:

Note this is for wood-burning fireplaces. Before lighting firewood add a few drops of essential oil.

Sweet Orange Humidifier:

Add a few drops of sweet orange essential oils to your humidifier. Note: Do not add essential oils to your humidifier if you suffer from asthma.

Verbena Vacuum:

On the outside of your vacuum's filter put a few drops of verbena essential oil.

Get Your FREE Bonuses Today!

FREE Fertility Advice from 'The Bringer of Babies'

Leading natural fertility specialist, Gabriela Rosa (aka The Bringer of Babies) has a gift for you. As a thank you for purchasing this book get your FREE "Natural Fertility Booster" subscription and discover...

- Easy ways to comprehensively boost your fertility and conceive naturally, even for women over 40;
- Natural methods to dramatically increase your chances of creating a baby through assisted reproductive technologies such as IUI, IVF, GIFT or ICSI;
- Simple strategies to help you take home a healthier baby;
- How to prevent miscarriages.

You will also receive the FREE audio CD "11 Proven Steps To Create The Pregnancy You Desire And Take Home The Healthy Baby of Your Dreams" a total value of $397!

Claim your bonuses at
www.NaturalFertilityBoost.com

Be quick, this is a limited offer.
(Your free subscription code is: ATCP)

Gabriela Rosa

Contacts and Resources

The Natural Fertility Solution
Take-Home Program

A whole person approach is fundamental to effectively restore and optimize natural fertility in both men and women.

Based upon this key observation and many years in private practice Gabriela Rosa developed the comprehensive and healing natural fertility approach she now successfully shares with couples worldwide. The Natural Fertility Solution *Take-Home* Program is based on Gabriela's proven fertility boosting strategies. This program focuses on enabling simultaneous optimization of the key areas (her 11 Pillars of Fertility), which most dependably will help couples to create the baby of their dreams, irrespective of their previous medical history.

Gabriela's approach has proven to be invaluable in helping prospective parents overcome fertility problems; increasing the chances of taking home a healthy baby as well as being able to prevent miscarriages or malformations and abnormalities (even for older couples). Despite its effectiveness in restoring fertility in delicate cases this is not its only application—her method is also an essential toolkit of *paramount importance* for those prospective parents who simply wish to prepare for the healthiest conception and baby—with the intention of giving their child the best possible start in life.

For more information on The Natural Fertility Solution *Take-Home* Program visit **www.BoostYourFertilityNow.com**.

Gabriela Rosa

WHAT ELSE IS ON OFFER?

From her Sydney practice, Natural Fertility & Health Solutions Gabriela and her team run The Natural Fertility Solution Program and also offer seminars and workshops as well as one on one and online consultations.

Other programs and modalities offered at Natural Fertility & Health Solutions include:

Programs

- Fertile Emotions Workshop and Whole-Person Fertility Support Groups;

- The PCOS Solution Program;

- The Endo(metriosis) Solution Program;

- Emotional Freedom Technique Workshops;

- Art Therapy;

- Vedic Meditation (transcendental technique);

Modalities

- Acupuncture

- Acupressure

- Chiropractic

Gabriela Rosa

- Classical Homoeopathy

- Craniosacral therapy

- Emotional Freedom Techenique

- Herbal Medicines

- Hypnotherapy

- Health & Life Coaching

- Myofascial Release

- Naturopathy

- Nutritional Medicine

- Osteopathy

- Relationship and Individual Counselling

Gabriela is available for interviews and can be contacted via the website www.BoostYourFertilityNow.com or through Natural Fertility & Health Solutions, PoBox 2342, Bondi Junction 1355 | 1300 85 84 90 or +61 2 9369 2655.

OTHER RESOURCES:

100% Pure Essential oils, Bottles, Jars etc

Australia

New Directions Australia

47 Carrington Rd
Marrickville NSW 2204 Australia
T: 612 8577 5999
F: 612 8577 5977
TOLL FREE: 1800 637 697
www.newdirections.com.au

Sydney Essential Oil Co

Unit 4, 2-10 Fountain S
Alexandria NSW 2015 Australia.
+61 2 9565 2828
www.seoc.com.au

Botany Essentials

39 Cranwell St,
Braybrook VIC 3019, Australia
+61 3 9317 9088
www.botanyessentails.com.au

Gabriela Rosa

USA

Wellington Fragrance Co.
33306 Glendale
Livonia, MI 48150

United States Toll Free (800) 411-3593
International (734) 261-5568 / (734) 261-5571 fax

Index